CLOUD CUCKOOLAND

CLOUD CUCKOOLAND

HARALD PENROSE

Illustrated by David Gibbings

An Airlife
CLASSIC

Copyright © 1981 Harald Penrose

First published in the UK in 1981
by Airlife Publishing Ltd
This edition published 1999

British Library Cataloguing-in-Publication Data
   A catalogue record for this book
   is available from the British Library

ISBN 1 84037 127 7

Printed in England by St Edmundsbury Press Ltd, Bury St Edmunds, Suffolk

Airlife Publishing Ltd

101 Longden Road, Shrewsbury, SY3 9EB, England
E-mail: airlife@airlifebooks.com
Website: www.airlifebooks.com

Contents

1 Questioning Prelude

All through an afternoon of early autumn I waited while heavy rain fell from dark grey castellated clouds. At last it slowed and stopped, leaving a blue-grey overcast and low scud scurrying before the wind; but away on the western horizon a promising patch of soft blue sky was revealed. I decided to go, started the engine of my scarlet-painted little biplane *Airymouse*, and lifted her into an evening made more brilliant every moment by the sinking sun. The scud became fire-crested, and the evening glow spread all across the western land – though north, east, and south, the countryside was shadowed and withdrawn. Slowly we climbed – 500 feet, 1,000, 2,000, and levelled off. This was the last flight I would ever make with her, for it was beginning to be too expensive to keep a private aeroplane. Within a few months I would be sixty-two and by making economies could at last retire from my lifetime's work in the aircraft industry. But what did the future hold for my new way of life? Was freedom a chimera or the final fulfilment?

As I flew, I thought of the many flights with *Airymouse* since relinquishing test-flying for a desk. They had been a happy bonus of hours in which I could gaze down at the countryside

7

and ponder its beauty and meaning. Everywhere the form and contour, the sweep of hill and vale, the fretted shape of encircling coastline had geological individuality, and yet continuing change to more and more arable and the spreading blotches of suburbia made the sky-view of the land very different from pre-war years. The old wild fields, the unspoiled downlands, and all that was once accessible only by horse and foot, had largely gone. In many places great brown areas of ploughed earth showed starkly – yet, hidden beyond the roads and lanes, broad vistas of dairy meadows still retained their network of hedges and infinitude of trees. Nevertheless the huge new motorways divorced from the life of the countryside, the factories, the encroaching towns and cities, all shouted an inescapable warning – for it requires no computer-compiled statistics to recognize from a small aeroplane the visual ecology and realize that the increase of mankind is overcoming the capacity of the land to produce sufficient subsistence. But it is not only England, I uneasily recollected: the octopus encroachment of an urban-orientated population in every country is overwhelming the vital civilization that was rooted in nature. All the world's environmental problems have that common factor – too many people.

Flying onward, solitary in the evening sky, I saw for a while only the empty, peaceful little fields of England and a scattering of cottages here and there: no people, just quiet countryside remote from the industrial ravages of man. Big business makes its millions as though this was a virtue excusing its reckless draining of the world's resources. From the serenity of the skies one sees the shadow drifting across the beauty of the earth, heralding the storm.

Airymouse hummed on, heading steadily into the golden west where the sun was filling the skies with a last flood of radiance. So peaceful this land – seemingly so timeless, so eternal. Could it really be in peril? Was I creating only an imaginary darkness? I thought of the quiet Wessex countryside; of the calm Cotswolds and their softly chiselled valleys and the great meadows

8

of the sheep pastures of old; of the windy, blunt green back of the Sussex heights; the dappled shadows sailing the grassy slopes of the Berkshire Downs; the Pennines brooding primitive thoughts amid storm-wrack; the austere, dark-walled table-land of the Mendips; wild geese settling on the marshlands of the Bristol Channel, East Anglia, and Moray Firth. And then I remembered that the downland tops had all but vanished under plough; that great quarries had been gashed into the chalks and rocks of many hills; gravel scooped by the million tons from open countryside; rivers dead with industrial and agricultural poison; the very air polluted by aircraft jet exhaust and a summer pall of smoke from needless stubble fires; even the oceans constantly contaminated with oil. These are the first indications of a peril no less dangerous than nuclear explosion.

It was not hard to imagine, as I looked through the pellucid atmosphere on which my wings sailed so confidently, that all this land spreading into the darkening distance was a battle-field. Though the kindlier hand of man was evident enough in the cultivated fields and secret farmsteads I had seen, the city of my destination was now visible, sprawling in unrelated patch-work far beyond its natural limits of a century ago. Petrol stations, dumps, sheds, power lines, factories, penetrated untidily into its tired and drab surrounding fields. Then rows of houses: thousand upon thousand people penned in anonymity aimlessly seeking distraction from themselves and indifferent to the future of the world. So few want to care – and yet at week-ends and holidays the cars stream from the towns in a mass-refugee movement seeking the inexpressible freedom that people miss, but in doing so they blight the very country-side to which they flee: too many people; too many for this little England.

Then I remembered that above me was the immensity and serenity of the skies: space extending limitlessly beyond the stars: infinity, eternity. Man runs his little instant in the eternal – his poignant moment of necessity born only to fade into the limbo of the universe. What has become of his humanity? Who is his god? Where is his salvation? He seems doomed to self-destruction.

The last glow had gone from the sky. In the gathering dusk I circuited the lamp-studded airfield, and straightened for my landing. *Airymouse* came sighing down. She settled gently as a butterfly upon the grass beside the tarmac apron. The world closed around us with a sense of shelter, safety, and the earth's comforting firmness and assurance. The hangar doors were open. I said good-bye to my staunch little aeroplane, and, in a sense, to the England I had loved.

A car was waiting. I drove off into the gathering dusk. What did the future hold, I wondered? I thought of my Dorset cottage where time stands still. Garden, field, and forest blend undisturbed: the wind murmurs in the trees: birds sing: buzzards soar. But what of sailing and flying? Did retirement on half-pay mark the end? Already the stars were glittering in the evening sky, ready to soften the darkness and make the world of realities subdued and remote. To-morrow was another day, ready to bring new promise I hoped.

2 Up and Away

More than a year had slipped away since my retirement. Time had no days of the week – just morning and daytime and night, the sun and the wind and the rain, and the hours scattering like leaves without need to look at the clock.

Unexpectedly a group of us had been presented with an ancient but delightful little low-wing monoplane named *Tipsy*. She seated two, side by side in an open cockpit, and was powered by an equally antique four-cylinder of a mere 65 h.p. The beckoning skies need no longer be ignored.

Though the pleasure of flying is only part of the complex integration of thought and reaction a pilot experiences, it was for me the compelling impetus behind all scientific flight investigation as a test pilot. To find the edge of danger with an

11

untried aeroplane was less a plunge into the unknown than a cautious step by step investigation that was my chosen job for twenty-five years, and its reward was a vision of the world and the vastness of the sky which I never dreamed of changing for more material rewards – for this was an integration with the very life and spirit of the universe.

It was no less so in my return to the simpler flying. On most occasions they were only short flights which took place on sunny days when the countryside was graced with a particular beauty. The first such flight was with that delightful relic of wartime days, an ancient Tiger Moth.

I liked the comfortable boxed-in feeling given by a biplane's two sets of wings, with their rakish struts and taut crossed bracing wires. There was an echo about it all of the golden age when all aeroplanes were light and glittering creations of varnished wood and doped fabric, that flew *on* the air instead of hurtl ng through it. What thousands must have had their introduction to the untrammelled skies in such machines. From the tight little cockpit they peered through the battering slipstream; saw the grass slide into a blur; felt the patter of wheels end in a last easy bound; watched the trees at the aerodrome's edge fling nearer, only to drop below – and suddenly realized with a thrill that this was flight! Regimented fields and trees would spread in widening expanse about their wings, reaching outward to the encircling line of horizon which, far away, separated land from sky. With unexpected detachment they would gaze at the little world of men, and all its mock formality of toy-like houses and streets, then glance at the spreading wings, and realize with what confidence they leaned upon the wind, rocking gently, lifting with easy buoyancy.

Musing on these things I looked over the padded rim of the Tiger Moth's cockpit, across the taut undulations of the canvas. The sun threw the shadow of my goggled head on the port lower wing. Tentatively I wiggled the ailerons. They bit the air promptly, rocking the machine as though it was directly actuated by the stick. Then, lifting the nose a little, I moved the control column smoothly across with a forward sweeping motion, my feet instinctively ruddering, and earth and sky rolled sideways until they changed place. With gentle forward pressure on the stick, I held the Tiger Moth on its back. The Sutton harness dug into my shoulders. A plume of petrol streamed from the tank vent on the centre-section, and the engine after a moment's running, spluttered and cut, the propeller windmilling like a slipping wheel.

In the sunny air my Tiger Moth went sliding for a brief ten seconds, with the fields and trees above my head – and then rolled off. With a bang or two, and a puff of smoke, the engine picked up. Tail held high to gather speed, we raced along, then pulled smoothly into a loop. The wind-song in the wires died as the nose tumbled backwards across the horizonless sky, only to find a wilder note as we dived towards the earth to recover normal flight.

The return to the aerodrome was as near as one can get to the poetry of movement. In the slowly sweeping curves of one turn after another, switch-backing from climb to dive and so to a long shallow glide, the Tiger Moth came sighing down. At 1,000 feet the idling engine was cleared with a short burst of throttle, and I turned in for final approach at 55 on the air speed indicator.

Instead of floating in just over the hedge I gauged for a touch-down near the aircraft parking place, half-way along the aerodrome. Absurdly enough it required deliberation to make the necessary high approach, for the same altitude with a highly laden, clean aeroplane would mean a hopeless overshoot. Yet for sheer pleasure in making approaches it would be hard to beat the Tiger. Give me a calm and lovely day, and it is a pastime the peer of sailing. So with the shameless delight of having put back the clock I aimed for the grass strip by the edge of the Control Tower tarmac. A moment more, the wheels were a foot off the ground – and I was gradually lifting the nose, holding off as long as possible the aeroplane's endeavour to sink onto the ground. A second or two of buoyant floating; then that last little drop, the simultaneous full backward flick of the stick, and the sudden rumbling of the tail-skid telling of a three-pointer. When the brakeless Tiger Moth stopped dead in line with its more modern brothers it added a cubit to my stature.

The light-weight *Tipsy* monoplane was just as pleasurable to fly, yet compared with the control response and stability of the robust Tiger Moth she was inferior as an instructional machine. Though the side-by-side cockpit looked tight for two, the second seat was not quite abreast but set slightly rearward to give sufficient shoulder room. There were separate interlinked rudder bars but the single centrally placed control column was shared, a detachable cross-bar handle projecting towards the passenger enabling his right had to be used, though he had to stretch across the cockpit to operate the second throttle behind the port seat. To safeguard against accidental stalling there was a permanently open slot built into each wing-tip leading edge, and elevator power was restricted by so limiting its upward movement that there was only just sufficient for landing. Although a drag flap was fitted to steepen the glide, she had no wheel brakes and that precluded touch-downs on tarmac runways because a grass surface was necessary to enable the tail-skid friction to pull her to a stop. This also made it tricky to attempt landing in small fields, for her run was longer than with the more lightly loaded *Widgeon* 'parasol' monoplane which I used to put down on any unimpeded 100-yard strip in days of old. Yet for a machine built in 1937 the *Tipsy* was a very advanced design, conceived by a Belgian pioneer, Oscar Tips, who with his brother Maurice had built his first flying machine in 1908. Between the wars he was one of the Fairey engineers, and operated their Brussels factory where he designed several light aircraft, including this little machine.

Before my retirement I had flown her on various occasions – but now she became my chief way of returning to that earlier way of life, and she winged me to endless enchantment. The heady rush of air flooding past the big curved windscreen restored that vivid sense of integration with the elemental world of sky and land and sea. Each little flight, however familiar the miniature of fields and trees and villages, was in its way a new adventure.

There was for instance a day in January when I attempted to fly to Weston-super-Mare. Though warmly clad in war-time fleece-lined leather, the air struck bitterly cold. Far across the countryside fields and copses glowed in the low winter sun, limning the trees and hedges in brown and black, and throwing long shadows in which the tracery of every branch was emphasized. Snow lay lightly scattered like sugar ice on the herbage beneath the sunless side of hedges, and powdered the tops of high ground. Away to the east it gleamed on the steep northern slopes of the Dorset hills where they rose firm and clear against an ice-blue sky.

Heading my aeroplane towards the low-lying plain of Sedgemoor I saw that the dyked ditches of the water-moors were brimming full, and the fields patched with gleaming pools and puddles. Presently the long ridge of the Poldens lifted above flooded Sedgemoor. Mallard and widgeon were flighting in small groups, but none of the usual teal. Everywhere lapwing clouded up from muddy fringes as though lifting from the water. As I flew onward, other flooded meres revealed the dark forms of numerous coots, their white head-blaze clearly visible, and on one waterway a score of swans were floating like water lilies spread across the surface.

But soon I discovered away to the north, where I must go, that a great snow-storm veiled the Bristol Channel, and the Mendips I must cross were topped by a white line of cloud twenty miles long, making the little space beneath it black and blind. Yet Glastonbury Tor stood sunlit in the intervening water-moors. Carefully I scanned the dark and threatening Mendip wall. There was no way through – not even a westward detour around the shores of the Bristol Channel, and certainly not over the top. Slowly my little monoplane swept round the wintry sky; then I steered for home, defeated yet undefeated.

Next day the snow had melted. The ploughed fields glistened. There were still great puddles in the soaked meadows. Here and there huge rain storms, black against a great space of dull grey sky, stalked like vast water spouts across the drowned countryside, each blotting out a huge area of land.

The air was rough, and my light aeroplane flew uneasily. Heavy down-currents jolted the wings, jerking me in my seat as we sped low above the floods. Wildfowl rose at our approach. Flying almost wing to wing, breasting the chasm of air in the same sky world, seeing identically the vista of drowned countryside and vastness of the surrounding sky storms, one finds truer understanding of bird life than when watching earthbound. From the ground all birds can be fascinating; beautiful; their song a delight: but the sky is their environment, and only when one joins them there does the natural relationship of bird and man become apparent.

So despite the storm-tossed atmosphere it was with a surge of interest and expectation that I followed a mixed flight of widgeon and mallard that had been disturbed by my encompassment of the flood. From the far side of their circling I kept them in view while we flew in opposite directions like a spinning wheel. Holding slightly lower altitude, my monoplane climbed three hundred feet in each circuit of forty-five seconds, which probably represented the maximum upward rate these wildfowl could maintain. At 2,000 feet I left them, for it seemed an intrusion to impose an extraneous will driving them higher and higher merely to see how far they would go and what they might do.

Gulls soared everywhere, hundred upon hundred, as we ranged the Godney plain and threaded the open spaces between each broad ten-mile column of deluging rain. When my wandering flight at last reached the grass airfield at Weston, long hidden behind one of the storms, a glory of sunlight flooded the countryside and turned the waters of the Severn to silvered satin brown.

But winter flying was a rare occasion. Spring, summer, autumn were the lures when the air had lost its bitter chill. On

most occasions there was no more than the simple pleasure of
starting the engine, taxi-ing on to the grassy strip of the 500-foot
high downland top of Compton Abbas airfield, stirring those
scarlet wings into life with opened throttle, and humming away
at gentle slant into the welcoming sky with the vista of Dorset,
Wiltshire, Somerset, and even far Hampshire, spreading ever
wider as I gazed at the quiet sunlit scene.

Sometimes I took a passenger. On one particular day my son
came with me. Heading south, we crossed the Dorset heights,
and spread before our wings was the distant fifteen mile
crescent of the Chesil Beach curving its vivid orange line of
demarcation between green slopes and silver sea. Suddenly he
pointed. 'Look – a fox!'

We watched it lope across the fields below, plodding up the
heights of Swyre Beacon, unhurrying but intent as it headed
towards the shore. We circled wide. Three miles away a
glimpse of scarlet caught our eyes, followed by a score or more
riders stringing across the road south of the great Iron Age
ramparts of Eggardon Hill. 'And there are the hounds!' called
my companion. 'They're a good mile nearer to us – and there is
the huntsman and his whipper-in.' Far behind, scattered along
the line, jumping an occasional fence or ditch, followed the rest
of the field, their cantering horses undulating like rhythmic
automatons.

We turned to the fox, a distinctive golden-red shape in the
sunlight. He had travelled some 600 yards in a couple of
minutes, but now he paused, nosed through a hedge, and
continued unhurriedly down the slope towards distant marshy
ground that was edged by the long pebble beach. On the other
side of the 400-foot hill behind him, hounds and huntsman had
crossed the quiet River Bride unseen by us, and were in the
adjacent lane, moving eastward, striving to raise scent. A brace
of hounds broke through its southern hedge: others followed,
the huntsman jumping a gate and curving wide behind them
then lifted horn to lips. On they went, struggling up the long,
rough northern slope of Swyre Hill, some of them lagging.

By now the fox was picking his way across the marsh where the low yellow cliffs of Burton Common dropped to the Chesil Beach and ended. Separating him from the stony beach was little Burton Mere. He contemplated its calm waters. Wildfowl, coots, and gulls floated undisturbed in this remote and secret place. He took a few steps forward – then swam across its 100-yard width, his long brush trailing. The wildfowl hardly stirred, but some of the gulls lifted and circled. Clambering out, the fox sat down on the edge of the beach, crossed it, and after a few moments padded along the low-tide mark, hidden from landward viewing by the 30-foot rise of the steep shingle ridge.

Again we banked in a wide sweep to relocate the hunt, the long length of foam-fringed shore sliding away and the green inland hills swinging into place in front of our whirling propeller. The pack had reached the coastal motor road that climbed with bold panoramic views from Bridport to Wears Hill, 700 feet above Abbotsbury. Clearly the hounds had lost scent in the mixed profusion of acrid tarmac and car exhausts. Huntsman and whip were trotting back and forth, marshalling the pack. A mile behind, the field had scattered widely – pink coats, green, black: horses cantering, horses walking. A few had found the river bridge and were seeking the gate to the fields and scrub of Swyre Hill.

We turned back to the Chesil Beach and its silver-rippled emptiness of sea, with Portland far to the east jutting its snake-head across the horizon. Maybe we had been with hounds and horsemen a mere five minutes – but the fox had vanished. We circled the Mere. Nothing. We flew a mile along the shore in the direction we last saw him walking carefree just out of reach of the lapping waves and fringe of foam. Nothing. We flew a beat or two across the wide strip of rough field and scrub between the hill-top road and broad pebble shore. Somewhere that hidden fox was chuckling as he lay contentedly at rest.

As on other occasions when I had followed a hunt by air, the fox had shown no sign of fear as he loped along – only an instinctive awareness that it was best to put distance between him and the sound of the horn and baying hounds. As we flew home I told my son, in shouted snatches of conversation above the wind's whistle and engine hum, how on one occasion I had circled high above a Somerset pack drawing a wood that fringed part of Merryfield aerodrome. Soon a fox broke cover, unscented by hounds, and walked quietly across the adjacent pasture; he paused where the main runway, redolent with jet exhaust, ended at the fence – then deliberately turned up the concrete landing strip, though that brought him on a parallel course with the wood less than 500 yards distant. I watched him trot towards the far end where the active hangars stood, but half-way came another runway intersection. There he stopped and faced the distant clamour, waited a full minute, and then I saw him swing away and depart steadily along the runway at right angles to the first, padding further and further from the hunt, wriggle through the far fence, and was lost to sight beneath my turning wing. Within a few minutes hounds streamed from the woods hot on his scent, and the hunt began moving around the wood. But when the pack reached the termination of the airfield's main runway, hounds were baulked by the overwhelming odour of burnt paraffin exhaust and ran hither and thither in confusion. Presently the hunts-man called them off, and hounds and horsemen departed to another copse far remote from my canny fox.

'Must be hundreds down there,' I said, sweeping my gloved hand across the broad vista of Dorset as we headed across the downland heights of Askerswell, aiming for Bulbarrow, the highest point on the steep north-easterly crown of the Dorset heights overlooking the quiet pastures of Blackmoor Vale. We flew like an arrow across the course of history; over downlands where the sabre-toothed tiger, the mammoth, and thousand upon thousand deer once roamed; and ancient man knapped flints dug from the chalkland heights where he made his home, living in circular huts of wood and turf in community groups guarded by the palisaded ditches of their great encircling defences. Everywhere time seemed to brood, watching the slow cycle of change. We followed the heights, heading towards the dominant twin hills of Hambledon and Hod, the earthworks of their fortress tops etched against the sky, and at their feet the River Stour wound its lazy way to Blandford Forum of the Romans and eventually to Poole.

We soared across the valley, passing high above the steep escarpment of Hambledon, and took the northern line of smoothly rising downland edging the wooded valleys of Cranborne Chase. Across the far horizon ahead lifted the Mendip range, and more distantly west loomed the Blackdown Hills and Exmoor. On the northern heights of the Chase was our landing strip on the edge of Melbury Down. We swept round with a last lingering look westward across the quietness of the Blackmoor Vale, curved into our approach glide, skimmed briefly across the turf, and settled like a homing bird.

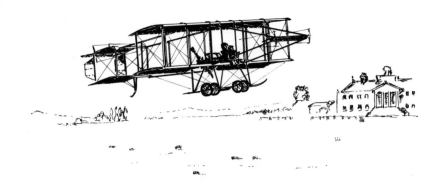

3 A Forgotten Air

There are ancient places with a slumbering aura of historical continuity, some of them inviolate, others lost beneath the layers of life as the years accumulate.

Slowly I drove through the Colindale entrance of what used to be Hendon Aerodrome, and headed towards the R.A.F. Museum where the railway embankment bounded the far side. On my right were the disguised but romantic sheds I remembered from earliest days when the doors flaunted the names of pioneer schools of flying: Grahame-White, Beatty, Deperdussin, Caudron; Blériot. On my left a wilderness of houses replaced the great grass field where, long ago, ancient monoplane and biplane uncertainly flew, piloted by the young adventurers and *conquistadores* of the dawning Air Age. Despite the visible change, there was still a feeling of the past – or was it that the men and their times lived only in my imagnation? The present is never really here: the stream of time flows on, and it is yesterday and to-morrow, the last minute and the next, which occupy the mind – for one is endlessly passing through the experience of living. And those pre-war pilots and constructors who used Hendon have almost all vanished from the face of the earth and are largely forgotten, although they were heroes of a great moment in the story of a world that has slipped away: a few of their aeroplanes alone remain as visible evidence, some of which are stored in the Museum on this historic Hendon site. But it was the men, and not the machines, who were so vital in writing that page of history which set the stage for journeys to the moon half a century later. One looks back and sees that what seemed unpredictable and unrelated events in one's lifetime were in fact the constituents of integrated history, pointing like a pathway towards some unimagined end, accumulating impetus as they reached towards every climax. As they recede we look back, and the veil parts a little, revealing a hint of purpose and of meaning.

The last time I landed an aeroplane at Hendon was a few years after World War II. The distinctive, almost triangular shape of this famous aerodrome was little changed from the years between the wars when I used to fly there for the R.A.F. Pageants and the displays held by the Society of British Aircraft Constructors; but even on that last occasion the houses of outer London were pressing closer.

My visit had been to a celebratory revival of Hendon days arranged by the *Daily Mail*. In a roped-off area was a collection of antique aeroplanes such as Hamel's racing Blériot, a Deperdussin which I remembered seeing as a lad race low down around chequered pylons on the airfield, a 'Horace' Farman pusher with walnut propeller and Renault engine, a Sopwith Triplane, a Camel, and an S.E.5a – thence to light aeroplanes which had prominence between the wars. History seemed to flow back from the scene, for time had given coherence to the story. I was standing by the 1915 Farman biplane, thinking how readily we commune with the past by occupying the very place where great events have occurred and famous men have lived, when a quiet voice broke into my thoughts:

'Do you remember how the wind used to hum in those wires?' said a tall man standing beside me. Nobody else was near. He was elderly but very erect, clasping an umbrella like a sword, and behind his gold-rimmed glasses the eyes were quick and bright. He was holding his bowler hat.

'Yes,' I answered, though I was only a small boy when I had seen Graham Gilmour and Gordon England flying a much cruder earlier version, and later had watched similar pre-Great War training biplanes make a wobbly circuit before nosing steeply down to land.

'It was wonderful,' he added quietly. 'We used to get up at dawn and fly our Boxkites all around Salisbury Plain while the morning air was calm. . . . There was a kind of music in the wires when we switched the engine off.'

In silence we continued standing there, the tall old man with a stranger of a later generation, both gazing at the ancient, delapidated Farman while, further away, a great crowd watched a display of jet fighters flashing past in a din like the breath of vengeance. But we had no eyes for modern aeroplanes.

'Upavon it was. . . . They made me one of the instructors. Delightful days. . . . Do you remember the smell of the burnt castor oil?'

I remembered as though it had been the nectar of the gods: the puff of blue smoke as the rotary engine fired, the glitter of spinning propeller, the slow drift of exhaust across the meadow, and its intoxicating, pungent perfume. Oh, did I remember!

The tall man pointed with his umbrella. 'That one has got a nacelle. We used to sit in the open on seats bolted to the lower wing. There was a marvellous view.' He glanced down quickly to see if I understood.

'Yes,' I said.

We reverted to silence, looking at the slender struts and the thin steel piano wires boxing the long and shallow wings whose scalloped trailing edge was like a bird's. How aerial, how delicately fragile, and though not particularly controllable, how responsive to every nuance of the air were those early aircraft – not projectiles hurtling through space, but aspiring to the skies like butterflies in the sunlight.

Presently my companion stirred from his reverie: 'Well, I'd better say good day and not stay talking of the past.'

He strode away – a distinguished, tall, spare figure – but perhaps, after all, a little bowed about the shoulders despite the upright military impress. I watched him heading towards the distant crowd, a lonely old man who had shaped the past: a great man almost forgotten, but known to his generation as 'Boom', and in history as Marshal and Father of the Royal Air Force, Baron Trenchard of Wolfeton in the County of Dorset.

The coincidences begin to link. I had a tattered rudder of the Boxkite which I had seen Graham Gilmour fly. On its time-stained brown fabric could faintly be discerned his pencilled description of the epic flight he and Eric Gordon England made that day of 12 April 1911 – the first *grande tourisme* by air.

They were instructors at the Larkhill flying-ground of the Bristol & Colonial Aeroplane Co. Ltd., located on a gently curving downland top on the edge of Salisbury Plain, not far from Amesbury and within sight of Stonehenge. Gilmour was twenty-three and England a boyish-looking twenty. Morning dawned cloudless, fresh as wine. No breeze stirred the springtime foliage. A great chorus of bird song filled the air. Through the wide opened casements of the George Inn at Amesbury the two young men leaned, confident the world was their plaything and that this was the day of days to explore it from the skies.

'Not enough wind to ruffle a thought,' said Gilmour, flyer of mercurial temperament and already the greatest exponent of trick flying although an airman of only a year's standing.

'Calm as a mill pool – just the day for it,' agreed the more stolid Gordon England who had become a test pilot of note though he had not yet been granted his aviator's certificate by the Royal Aero Club.

By half past six the pair had driven in Gilmour's grey two-seat Panhard to the flying-field sheds. Already the doors had been opened, and blue-overalled mechanics were pushing out the School's Boxkite biplanes – translucent-winged creations, with slender struts separating top and bottom wing and boxing the four booms of the tail outriggers cross-braced by scores of glittering wires, the woodwork gleaming yellow with transparent copal varnish that reflected the bright morning sun.

Rocking on the elastic cord springs which bound the stub axles of the twin pairs of wheels tranversely to the sweeping skids, the aeroplanes rolled to a halt in front of the sheds, their single-acting ailerons drooping vertically. Men fussed around, thrumming a tight wire, adjusting a turnbuckle, checking engine valve clearances, pumping the tyres of the wire-spoked wheels, pouring petrol from red-painted *Shell* cans into the aeroplane's brightly polished copper tank, and filling the second tank with castor oil. Gilmour and England sprawled on the turf, watching while they half listened to the larks and lived the secret anticipation every pilot experiences.

Presently their aeroplane was ready. They stepped into overalls, tucked in their scarves, and pulled caps with peaks reversed firmly about their ears. They clambered from wheels to steps on the nearest chassis strut, thence to seats exposed tandemwise upon the lower wings six feet above the ground. No windscreen or nacelle gave protection, nor were such adjuncts necessary with a machine which, for all its 50 h.p., flew at speeds no greater than a racing pedal-cyclist could achieve.

England made himself comfortable on the raised rear seat. Horizontally behind him were the fuel and oil tanks placed high to give gravity feed to the star-like seven-cylinder Gnôme rotary mounted behind its integral walnut propeller above a recess in the lower wing trailing edge. He reached back and checked that the cocks were on.

His companion settled at the controls. A strut which could be grasped by his free left hand gave an illusory sense of security – for safety belts had not been invented, and his seat was on the wing leading edge, poised over an abyss of space on a ladder-like frame carrying the rudder bar. Ahead, the view was splendidly unencumbered except for the wide front elevator framed on either side with a triangular supporting structure running to top and bottom wings. To left and right, above and below, stretched the broad flax-covered wings, whose struts and cross-wires gave the flimsy wooden fabric box the dignity of pillared cloisters.

Gilmour set the engine levers, mounted on the nearest interplane strut, and threw a quick glance astern. A mechanic ducked under the tail booms and with a shout of 'switch off' spun the propeller. The bright steel cylinders whirled with hollow clicks of their valves as they sucked in the priming mixture. Now that the moment was near, Gilmour and England felt a wave of exultation – for they had discovered the universal truth that flying is a process of repeated reincarnation into regions pure and free where no earth bound will is absolute but the spirit of the universe reigns supreme. Not that either of them, that spring morning, could have put his happiness into words: sufficient that in a few more moments they would mount dream-like into the air and find the adventure and fulfilment of renewed experience.

'Contact,' cried the mechanic.

'Contact,' blithely answered Gilmour twisting half round in his seat to make sure that men were clinging to the tail outriggers to restrain the machine, for wheel chocks also had not yet been invented.

The mechanic, with both hands on a blade, tested his balance, then with a mighty heave swung the propeller. In a cloud of blue smoke the engine purred into erratic life, whirling metallic silver and spitting oil. The whole structure of the aeroplane tremored. England sniffed appreciatively at the burning castor lubricant as though it was the most vital ingredient of the fresh morning air.

In a crescendo of bursts of power the engine purred and spluttered. There was no slow running: it was either stop or go, for control was largely by switching on and off. The wings swayed at each acceleration, and the mechanics holding on to the tail struts strained against the pull, their overalls flapping like flags in the slipstream. Then Gilmour waved. The men let go – and the swaying biplane trundled over the downland

grass, slowly gathering strength, made a little hop corrected by
a jerking tilt of the front elevator, began to float its ailerons
level, waggled the twin rudders, steadied, and in another fifty
yards had left the ground. Like a great moth, like a soft flying
owl, this creation of magic white wings slowly rose with brittle
metallic song – a hundred feet and then another, and canted
gently to circuit the flying field. The group of mechanics craned
their necks to watch it floating past, as it headed south, droning
like a hive of bees.

Gilmour, lips compressed against the pressure of the wind,
glanced at his leather-cupped wristwatch: 7.30 a.m. The
dwarfed grey circle of Stonehenge came sliding under the front
elevator as though to remind them that other men had different
gods; but the couple in the aeroplane, using the spear-like spire
of Salisbury as guide, were scanning the rolling downlands and
the pattern of dusty white roads for sight of the railway line they
must follow to Yeovil, where they hoped to land for oil and
petrol on a field at Martock westward of the town. . . . Maybe it
was then that the gods laughed quietly and began to weave a
thread of coincidence through the fabric of the years.

Ah! But the rhapsody of soaring through the present that was
then; the thrill of adventure in that dawning of flight; the
carefree winds of heaven on the brow of youth; sunlight,
freedom, the buoyancy of wings sublime as an angel's, slowly
floating across the paradise of England – that was the experience of Gilmour and England when man was first achieving the
reality of his long-cherished dream to see the world from the
viewpoint of a bird. Pleasure drove away all other thought.
There lay the land, gently fair with trees and fields and streams,
the beauty of uncounted ages unveiled at last. How could they
know that life was but a moment's recognition in the eternity of
time? With promise of ever new revelation, the far horizons
beckoned on and on. Contentedly the Gnôme purred its droning, hypnotizing song above the howl of bar-taut wires, while
the green landscape flowed smoothly past three hundred feet
below, empty except for an occasional field labourer staring up

with the same uneasy wonder as the thousand sheep which dotted the downs.

The Cathedral's spire had drawn almost abeam, and at their feet the two young men saw the little township of Wilton, still asleep behind the great house of the Earls of Pembroke. Athwart their feet stretched the black track of the railway. Gilmour turned right handed, intent on following. Maps were useless in the streaming wind whipping around them. The course must be memorized – and they had no compass.

'This is it,' shouted the pilot, as they peered eagerly about.

Perhaps the broad white wing obscured the lateral view, or in the excitement of this novel voyage they forgot the second line that branched nearby. Everything was so new and strange. They went floating sublimely on: following the rail track which headed a little north before turning to what seemed west, judging by the sun. Oh youth, youth, questing new truths that were long discovered only to be lost again!

Cattle, unused to droning noises from above, stirred fearfully and fled before them. Chickens ran in scatter-brained dismay. From house and cottage men and women would appear and stare transfixed at the white-winged apparition. Gilmour waved; England stared down, gulping at the rush of air. Forgotten was the noise of flight, the rasp and roar. The Gnôme purred unfalteringly, and the propeller flashed and glowed as it tirelessly whirled. But after half an hour of flying, Gilmour's buoyant confidence felt a first faint disquiet, for the railway had swung further to the right. A moment later he realized they were lost. The hills were lifting into escarpments differing from his recollection of the coloured contours of the map they had studied the evening before, and there was a large town ahead where none should be.

'Must have followed the wrong line,' he shouted over his shoulder. 'Any idea what that place is?'

'Might be Warminster,' yelled England.

Gilmour swung the Boxkite round. The white wings and prow-like front elevator sedately canted. A dusty road threaded the downland southward.

'We'll follow that,' said Gilmour. 'It's bound to bring us to the other railway.'

On and on – fly with rapturous wing towards the unknown; scale heights no longer unattainable; reach towards the stars. England smiled at Gilmour's back, wondering what his companion thought; but Gilmour, intent on the slowly changing view, conscious only of the slow surge of his wings and the rhythm of the engine, had for the moment forgotten he was not alone.

For fifteen minutes more they climbed slowly in company with the road across the downs, but as they crossed the steep declivity of Whitesheet ridge a town of gold-hued stone that lay below dragged them to alertness from the timelessness with which flight enfolds the mind. The steeply descending road merged with another that led through the town and away westward.

'Along there?' called Gilmour.

'Try it,' shouted England.

Five minutes later they saw a long plume of smoke moving parallel with them but faster, six miles away on their left. 'I think it's the South Western,' came Gilmour's voice as he turned towards it and followed the train.

'Probably,' replied England, 'and that must be Templecombe where the Bristol to Poole line crosses it.' Methodically he checked the fuel level in the vertical glass gauge behind him, then shouted to the pilot that it was getting low.

'We'll land to ask the way and fill up,' called Gilmour. 'I'm going to try for that meadow by the station.'

He tilted the Boxkite sharply down, the front elevator pointing at a large field between road and railway. The rotary faded into what seemed stark silence after its comforting hum, only to break into a series of stuttering snarls as Gilmour switched it on and off. In what was fashionably termed a *vol piqué* they plunged down at a steep but stately 35 m.p.h., gauging the speed by the steady moan of the bracing wires. High above the near hedge the Boxkite slanted, travelling a bare fifty yards before it was skimming the ground as Gilmour flared the flight path, and a moment later the twin pairs of wheels rasped the grass and the machine settled with gentle bumps and tail still floating high, ran a mere thirty yards until the skids dragged, and slowed to a stop. There it rested in the sunlight like a great white butterfly with wings outspread, trembling from the last erratic spurts of the switched-off engine.

Gilmour turned in his seat and grinned at his passenger. 'Wonder if they'll give us breakfast at that house?' he said.

Ninety minutes later a small boy of seven, leaning from the corridor window of a train waiting at Templecombe station, heard the reverberating, accelerating drone of an engine quite different from the few motor-cars and motor-cycles he had seen. Then, miracle of miracles, a great aeroplane, white winged and glittering, lifted with cavernous din above the tops of the trees and sailed slowly and splendidly past. Along the length of the train scores of windows slammed down and rows of faces peered into the sky.

'An aeroplane – an aeroplane!' cried everyone. 'You can see the men in it!'

Standing on tiptoe, leaning far out, the boy stared and stared until the white wings were lost to sight and the purring engine faded to the faintest hum and then was gone. In the carriages and on the platform everyone was talking excitedly, glancing occasionally into the skies as though they might find the aeroplane still there. Presently the station-master strolled by.

'That was Mr. Graham Gilmour, the famous aviator, with a passenger,' he told everyone. 'They landed to have breakfast at Freyern Court, and are touring the West Country.'

My father smiled at me. 'Well, youngster,' he said. 'What do you think of that? It seems your birthday's going to be quite memorable, what with this and sailing when we get to Swanage.'

'It was a biplane,' I said with conviction. 'But I wish it had been Mr. Gustav Hamel because he flies monoplanes.'

Handsome young Hamel was a friend of my aunt, and I had his picture framed upon my bedroom wall. I saw my parent hadn't quite comprehended the importance of what I said, so I added: 'You know – a monoplane like the one Monsieur Blériot flew.'

My father gravely nodded. 'Yes, of course – your friend Hamel. Perhaps one day you'll see him too . . . but sit down now – the train is overdue to start.'

In the distance I heard the guard blow his whistle. From far away I felt the train jerk into motion and accelerate to its rhythmic thumpety thump. The telegraph poles flicked past in a blur. Blindly the sun-enchanted countryside spun round. But the interest of the journey to reach the sea, for which I had so long looked forward, had diminished. I was a small boy, curled in a corner seat, wrapped in a dream of wings.

Meanwhile Gilmour and Gordon England were following the railroad south towards Blandford, seeking Eastbury Park – not far from Tarrant Rushton where Sir Alan Cobham established Flight Refuelling after the Second World War.

'There's a beautiful girl who lives at The Manor,' said that gay Lothario, Gilmour, whose practice it was to know the owner of every such estate. He and his friend duly found her house, lunched there, and gave the girl a flight. Early that evening, the two young pilots again started for their Martock destination, keeping to the railroad more rigorously than ever, but at Templecombe, where they changed course to follow the South Western Railway, they found that the west wind had freshened considerably, giving negligible forward speed, so they decided to land near Henstridge station. As Dallas Brett records in his *History of British Aviation:* 'There they put up for the night, and on going to the machine in the morning, found that the field in which they had landed was too small to take off with two up. Gilmour accordingly flew the biplane out and landed in another field a mile away to pick up Gordon England.

They reached Martock safely and stayed there all day giving exhibition flights. Earl Poulett invited them to dinner at Hinton St. George, and the dashing Gilmour dispatched Gordon England by road, so that he could himself follow by air with a lady passenger. He had intended to land in the park, but when he arrived he found too many trees and golf bunkers to make it attractive, so resolved to put the aircraft down on the lawn in front of the house. He accomplished this safely, but overran on the smooth turf and carried away one of the fences.'

But the game of consequences continued down the years. Graham Gilmour was fatally injured ten months later when a wing of his Martin Handasyde monoplane collapsed on a day of great turbulence. A decade later I became acquainted both with Handasyde and Gordon England, and continued to meet the latter from time to time, always finding him to be the same vivid character, his blue eyes flashing as he recounted incidents of early days.

It also happened that I joined the lady of the flights, Mrs. Farquharson, at her eightieth birthday party – a still beautiful and lively lady, undoubtedly the gracious châtelaine to her village of Tarrant Royal, and she described to me the thrill and delight of her flight with the dashing Gilmour. Earlier, her nephew had given me one of the Boxkite rudders bearing the diary of that week-end tour.

More than ten years later, the succeeding Earl Poulett, finding he was taxed out of existence and that the rising cost of labour made it impossible to maintain his ancient estate in the protective manner of his forefathers, decided to sell out and live elsewhere.

He rang me not long after I retired , and said he 'had part of an old aeroplane I might like to see, for it had crashed on the lawn when he was a boy. I found that what he had was the other rudder of the Boxkite displayed in a glass-topped case which had kept it perfect. While a great removal van was being packed with the family heirloom pictures, he showed me his Inigo Jones house, and the lawn, unchanged, on which Gilmour had landed, watched by the household. Outside the garden there were certainly meadows where he would have had more room, but Gilmour must have decided that would have been a reflection on his skill. So the lawn in front of the mansion, giving little more than a hundred yards as he came over the trees, was his target; but on the grass of the last third of its length was a statue, and it was in avoiding this that he ran into the iron fence beyond. Rather than risk a marginal take-off after repair, the Bristol chairman insisted the machine must be dismantled and returned by road, thereby adding to the chagrin of his chastened firebrand, Gilmour. One rudder was given to the present Earl's father, and the other made a new excuse to visit the beautiful Mrs. Farquharson and give it to her. Thus in the course of time I acquired both rudders, and that was the reason for visiting Hendon again, recapturing this memory, and handing both relics to the R.A.F. Museum.

I looked at the spread of new houses, uniformly conforming with to-day, marshalled by the hundred on what had once seemed the jousting field of many a young man seeking the skies with untried wings. All that history gone: an alien air, except for the whisper of ghosts: the stutter and bark of engines forgotten: the gasp of the crowd unheard as Chevillard whirls his Farman biplane into a corkscrew roll: no roar of cheers as Cody sails low past the white rails of the enclosure on his triumphant machine. All gone – like the great house of the Pouletts: gone the clatter of hooves on the cobbles: no more bejewelled Countesses in satins, the glitter of chandeliers extinguished, the portraits and armour vanished, the glories of a great family unimaginable except for the effigies of knights and their ladies in the Poulett chapel nearby. Only the wind in the yews of three centuries remains to sigh.

4 With Cry of Curlew

I had taken off from Compton Abbas hill-top airfield with the scarlet little *Tipsy* and set her climbing towards the Somerset moors. A thousand feet above a late autumn countryside etched with rust-red trees, she droned placidly west by north. It might have been a scene on Mars at which I gazed – yet only a fortnight earlier the trees and fields possessed the green residue of summer, and gave no hint that winter's brittle blackness soon would net the earth. But now there was this unreal flaming of a familiar landscape made strange and memorable because the peak of autumn is so transient that even from the sky it may pass unperceived year after year.

A contrasting sombre ceiling of grey cloud and many scattered dark curtains of slanting rain emphasized the fiery quality of the landscape. A first its brilliant rufous beauty was entrancing, but presently my gaze turned towards the softer tones of distance where the broad olive-green lowland of Somerset, criss-crossed with endless dykes, spread wide – devoid of trees save a few bare alders and willows. Gradually the flat meadows drifted towards my wings, and far beyond them a new horizon loomed where the Mendips marched mistily across my path.

Anciently reclaimed from brackish lakes left by a receding

sea, the succession of seered brown squares of grassland bore the fissured impress of so many vanished streams that, from the height at which I was flying, the entire area of four hundred square miles seemed like a great estuary from which the tide had ebbed. Soon winter would revert these water-moors to a series of vast floods, where wading birds and migrant duck and geese would once more gather by the hundred thousand. But to-day, though flocks of lapwing twinkled distantly and rushes of starling fled at my oncoming, there were only a few swans sedately swimming in the long straight draining rhynes, and a brace of heron winnowed away against the wind on slow grey wings.

Conditions were far from ideal for bird watching. Bright light is necessary to illuminate coloured plumage for quick recognition. Instead, a south-west wind whipped dull clouds endlessly across the countryside. Where a torrent of rain fell through descending air a tilted canopy of cloud dragged low across the ground. Most of them I dodged, but eventually a passing downpour spread across my path, hemming in the aeroplane, and for a few minutes blotted everything except the ground immediately beneath.

Lower and lower the opaque veil of rain drove *Tipsy* until we were dangerously low for hidden steeple or tree. With drumming rattle, pellets of torrential downpour rebounded from wings and windscreen. Goggles upraised, I peered with stinging eyes through the cold draught for sight of the Mendip range lest we ran blindly into its wall-like sides. Presentiment growing, I turned the aeroplane cautiously towards a rift mistily opening ahead. It grew brighter, and the dark arrows of rain parted to reveal the rocky spur of Brean Down, an outpost of the Mendips, jutting into the brown flood of the Bristol Channel. Each side of the sea-girt promontory, acres of glistening mud had been gouged by the ebb into fantastic traceries of fern-like patterns burnished into silver trickles of shining water. Here was the dynamic model of the grass-covered water-moors over which I had been flying.

The fire and bronze of autumn became forgotten as *Tipsy* crossed the coastline into pale sunlight shining through a cloud rift. The glazed brown sea and patterned miles of mud prompted me to throttle back, and I came gliding into an unexpected sanctuary mud-world of quietly babbling birds. I steered towards the firm line of the ebb-water level and swept round the wooded headland that shelters Weston-super-Mare. What seemed scattered tufts of seaweed in Sandy Bay became thronging wild fowl and curlew scattering right and left. Sweeping *Tipsy* into a circle, her tilted wing-tip a few feet above the mud, I watched the duck flotillas rise and settle, only to rise again and fly off-shore. I turned back seaward to Weston Bay. Gulls cascaded from the cliffs of Sprat Beach below Brean Down. Scores of shelduck sprang from the distant mud, defying chase by swinging individually away on rapid wing. A flock of curlew took the air, lifting on angled wings higher and higher, and disappeared over the beetling neck that linked Brean Point to the mainland. In quick pursuit, I turned the aeroplane, leaping the peninsula with fractional pull on the controls, and the vista abruptly changed from corrugated mud and shining puddles to a view of the Mendips rising massively against the dark sky away to my left. Though it was a dramatically enlarged storm-torn vista that we gained, the flighting curlews speeding across Berrow Flats were instantly visible. As I slanted towards them I could see that the pointed tips of their supple-wristed wings flailed down and forward with powerful thrust, then whipped up like a lash twice as fast for the next stroke, driving down and forward again and again as they confidently sought escape from the noise of my pursuit. With easy grace they eluded me, banking steeply on a turn far too sudden to follow. My wings went vertical, but the curlews took a much narrower circle and swept from sight as the cliffs of grey Brean loomed again, a bare two hundred yards beyond the whirl of my propeller. They had scattered like chaff on the wind. Nothing but luck brought one of the escapers in sight as I finished my turn. He was streaking through the air with urgent strokes, barely a hundred yards ahead. I snatched back the throttle.

Steadily decelerating, the aeroplane drew towards the curlew, then held station using partial power. Every movement was clear as though I held him in my hand. A glance at the airspeed indicator showed 52 m.p.h. – a fantastically fast speed for such a bird. We were at 200 feet, and showed a just perceptible climb. Fascinated, I watched the curlew's wings sweeping up and down with beautiful, clean-cut action, rhythmically elegant as a leaping leopard. I counted the wing-beats: thirty-five in 3½ seconds – three times that of a gull flying unsoarable air. So intent was I on the curlew that I scarcely realized we had turned inland, away from the shore. He flew in little zig-zags. Once or twice the bird tried a bigger sweep, but, finding I dogged his course, he re-orientated eastward within a few seconds.

Five minutes passed, during which we climbed to 600 feet. I let him draw ahead. The bird eased his flailing wings but began to gain height faster. Our speed had dropped to 42 m.p.h. Higher we lifted, gaining altitude foot by foot. Steeper rose the foothills of the Mendips like a barrier across our path; yet presently we had risen so high that the smooth ochre-coloured top was two hundred feet beneath. Like a giant wedge, with long axis lying eastward, the great upland range reared boldly from the Somerset plain. Along the steep southern escarpment the curlew flew with unfaltering beat, the aeroplane threshing noisily astern, a hundred yards away. Slowly the altimeter rotated. We crossed Loxton Gap, and presently were well over 1,000 feet, the Mendips no longer looming mightily but flattened by our height to a panorama of pitted turf, black stone walls, and steeply tumbling edge.

How much longer could the curlew maintain such speedy flight, I wondered; and why in trying to avoid me did he fly so steadfastly from the sea? By now I had been tailing him full ten minutes, during which he could have got away at any moment. Bird of high moorland that he was, he needed only a quick drop to reach rocks and rough hill-top grasses which would give familiar shelter. Instead he maintained his amazing speed.

Suddenly the answer came. Two hundred feet below his powerfully beating wings a distant gull materialized steadily soaring towards us along the hill, his wings widespread and still. For a moment I did not realize the connection between his mode of flying and the curlew's.

Only a little distance above the Somerset plain, saturated clouds still were precipitating rain in half a dozen darkly slanting showers, each some five miles in diameter. I remembered how tired the air was, lacking dynamic buoyancy because of a low temperature inversion. How then could a gull manage to soar? Seated in my cockpit I could feel the rippling slipstream on my face so keenly that I had forgotten a real wind blew and was deflected sufficiently upward by the lateral hill slope to enable a bird to soar on planing wings. I looked at the curlew still beating onward in eager headlong flight at speed far higher than his normal cruising. The secret was simple. Like the gull, he knew the advantage of that invisibly welling up-current – but rather than utilize it for soaring, he employed the upward energy to give still greater speed than feasible in static air from the mere thrusting of his powerful pinions. Like the cranes I had seen above Greece, like all migrating birds in the thermal currents of anti-cyclonic weather, he did this by adding to his speed the impetus of a shallow dive in which his rate of descent was exactly neutralized by the up-current. I could at last appreciate that he was using utmost muscle and will to outdistance this relentless, noisy shadow that dogged him, unaware that my aeroplane would never tire.

Suddenly he was there no more. I had not looked away, nor even blinked, but during the quick black-out of concentrated thought the curlew disappeared into empty air. For a few moments I searched for him in a landscape grown bleaker by the absence of this little breath of life, then I turned *Tipsy* on course for home. As we droned along, my thoughts drifted from a world where rain was quenching the fire of autumn, and I saw the land re-born after winter sleep. I imagined the curlew flying with the spring, questing from winter mudflats to the nuptial moorlands, heaths, and saltings that presently would echo to his longing cry: *kour-lee, kour-lee.*

That evocative call stirs the ghosts of memory, so that I see again the wildfowl on Suffolk's quietly flowing Orwell as the flood inches secretly across the mudflats. A keen east wind sweeps in from the sea, but in the grassy hollow where we shelter the rising ground wards off its bitter touch. Muffler tucked into overcoat, and cap pulled firmly down, my father cautiously peers over the top at the vista of mudbanks and stream. We had left his small car a long way back, walked a field or two, and jumped a ditch before finding the low shore where the saltings still seemed uncertain whether they had been fully won from the water. On the far side of the river the ground rose higher, with fields and trees sharpened by that brilliance and lucidity which only the rain-washed clarity of East Anglian skies can give. It was a landscape of solitude and timeless pulse, where the unrelenting charge of tattered clouds seemed to emphasize the frailty of man's hold.

The air was full of quiet sound: brittle rustle of long grasses and reeds, soft breathing of tide and sucking mud, wail of gulls above muted babble and whistle from wildfowl scattered not far away – but clear above all was the cry of curlews. Wariest of birds, they rise at slightest provocation, yet, once airborne, they flew with bold, deliberate wings not far above our heads. Round and about they curved through the air and round again, one or two diving low only to tower steeply with exaggerated beats before checking almost to a standstill by quick forward thrust of pinions. Smoothly dropping in stalled flight, long wings spread and still, curlew after curlew utters a charming, bubbling song. Rising and falling, swooning to the ground, yet always recovering just in time, they unexpectedly change the mode of flight to powerful, measured beating, imparting to the air the very vigour of their gladness – while a female here and there lifts her curved Egyptian beak and watches. *Kour-lee, kour-lee, wi-wi, wi-wi, kour-lee* implore the males in the wild music of their ritual aerial dance.

'Pity I disturbed them,' the old man whispers as he lowers his head beneath the swaying grasses. 'It has made the widgeon uneasy.' Even as he spoke, the wildfowl, in squadron after squadron, leapt into flight with a great hiss of wings, circling wide across the dark water to settle further out, the widgeon descending last. Their pleased whistling, and the soft piping of teal mingling with the quack of mallard, quickly made a renewed background to the wild cry of the curlews.

'Beautiful,' murmured my father.

From sky and water the voices continued calling. We sat and watched and listened – mostly in silence, for there was little need to speak. The wilderness magic held an intense, all enveloping sway. Attunement to this basic thing of birds and quiet water unconsciously gave deeper understanding of each other, bridging the gulf that separates young men and their seniors into different outlooks. Covertly I studied my father, suddenly seeing him as a man who had nearly had his day – though it was beyond all comprehension that I should write these words at a time when I am much older than he was then.

'When you retire next year, you'll be able to do a lot more of this again,' I presently said.

His keen blue eyes twinkled. 'No need to console me,' he laughed. 'There's no point in living in the past, and certainly not in trying to repeat it. . . . Days like this become a kind of happy treasure and not things of vain regret. . . . No, my boy, I'm going to spend my remaining years in quite a different way.'

'How?' I demanded – and the living background of curlews protested with their wild *kour-lee*.

'All this kind of thing is part of one's fulfilment,' and he gestured broadly with a sweep of his hand, 'Nevertheless it is man's destiny, and I believe his happiness as well, to go on struggling – not just give up. So I'm standing for Parliament at the next election.'

'Whatever for?' incredulously I asked. Politics seemed a far

40

call from the way of life he loved – a difficult, heartless, disillusioning road.

'For peace, the joy of labour, and content,' he firmly replied. 'They are every man's right.'

'Politics are a placard,' I said.

'Then I would like to try and invest them with reality. . . . I will affirm the faith of my belief with the tongue of a true Cornishman – for Parliament should be the voice of the people and not a hidden cabal or a clique of place-seekers.'

'Why waste your time when you could fill the days with things you like: travel abroad, books, the arts – the lot? Why not take it easy?'

'Perhaps it's like your test flying. There must be days in those aeroplanes when it is difficult or even dangerous, and you have to struggle with yourself to bring the task to a fitting conclusion. . . . In a sense, life is a story book of which the things we do are chapters. I need to bring a sense of deeper purpose to mine before the bell tolls for the last time.'

In that bird-haunted silence of crying curlews I felt saddened at the shadow cast by the old man's final words. All too late I had matured to a point in his last few years at which I began to understand him. We had experienced many things together, yet sometimes had been strangely separate, each building his own vision of the same truth. But now I saw that truth goes inward as well as outward: at one moment man is the pattern himself, and at the next he views it from afar hoping to remould it to new purpose. Perhaps imagination at last had pricked my heart and mind to fuller awakening, so, in that instant, a sense of understanding took firmer hold. I saw life extending in a chain-reaction beneath and beyond the physical appearance by which man recognizes it. As though in materialization of my thoughts there came high above the estuary a great arrow of birds flighting north.

'Look! Wild geese!' I exclaimed. 'They've left it pretty late.'

Together, we watched them flying with beautiful precision, long necks outstretched, as with easy strokes they swiftly fled the springtime promise of English shores, seeking the land of their birth. Northward they passed – northward whither? Their whispering wings had secret purpose. From what past they came no man would know – or what their future. Nor, as the birds looked down, would they themselves care, for we, as men, were incomprehensible. Our world had struggles and hates, tyrannies and treacheries in form unknown to them – yet bird and man inherit the same fair earth which gives them life and sustenance and love. Nothing could touch the high wild eagerness of the geese as they flew with music throbbing in their great grey wings, indifferent to us watching far below with intent, upturned faces. Swiftly their echelon formation diminished to invisibility in the northern sky, leaving only a rustling, silver-blue emptiness above the distant trees.

'They can feel the spring in their blood,' my father said. 'An incalculable succession of springs has made stepping-stones across the world for them. No barriers hold them It is like the spirit of man – questing for a goal with purpose that he does not fully understand, yet perpetually discovering new worlds. In a way I'm glad you're involved in that kind of work – though I wish it wasn't flying.'

That hour with the curlews and wildfowl was the last we ever had of bird watching together. Indeed I only saw him once more before his unexpected, sudden end – the last dream unaccomplished. Our homes were two hundred miles apart – yet by the long arm of coincidence it was not far from this same Orwell that I had to make an emergency parachute jump some months later, when escaping from a prototype aeroplane after a wind had broken off in a dive. That evening I stayed at his home, explaining my earth-grimed clothes by saying I'd had a fall. After supper and desultory talk of this and that, and his expectation of becoming an M.P., I went to bed but could not sleep because my mind kept churning the sequence of events leading to the structural failure of my aeroplane. Half-wakeful fantasies made me think that I had got out too soon, despite the obvious evidence of the mass of wreckage filling the sky.

In the middle of the night I stirred from an uneasy doze to hear the old man padding down the stairs and talking for some time to people at the door. I had forgotten that newspapers employ importunate reporters who do not hesitate to intrude on privacy for the sake of a story. Presently I heard the door close and my father slowly returning. Outside my room he paused, then softly entered. Quickly I closed my eyes and pretended to sleep. For a while he just stood there, close to my bed – then bent down and gently kissed my cheek as though I was still a small boy. Then he stole away.

Sometimes the forlornly haunting cry of curlews drifts down as they pass unseen in the dawn mist above my Dorset cottage, stirring old and hidden longing. Yet I would have it no other way. It is better to remember.

5 Bubble of Air

Unexpectedly a new vista was offered – to drift across the summer landscape in a hot-air balloon.

Recently I had been corresponding with an enthusiast who was seeking information on flying a balloon in tropical climates, at great heights, with a view to securing a long distance record. Then it transpired that among his engagements he was booked to ascend at a village fête not far from my home, and I was invited to join as crew. Ever since seeing my first balloon, as a lad just before the Great War, I had hoped to fly in one. On that occasion I was walking the sheep-cropped Berkshire Downs with my parents when a great golden-brown orb lifted slowly like a rising moon above the hill slope ahead and drifted towards us, its trail rope dragging to reduce speed. Though I had seen many aeroplanes flying, and had even climbed into the pilot's seat of a Blériot, this huge creation seemed the epitome of aerial magnificence as it silently drew near as though from another world.

'Look! There are men in it,' I exclaimed, pointing at the

basket suspended from the lace-like network enclosing the spherical envelope.

'Of course there are,' my male parent gruffly said, 'and don't you dare touch that rope or you'll be carried away.'

One of the army officers aboard called down with cupped hands: 'Where are we?'

'Near Lambourn and heading for Newbury,' my father shouted.

'Thanks,' came a receding voice as the glittering apparition drifted away.

Balloons were filled with coal gas in those days, but I knew that the very earliest, with which the Montgolfier brothers in 1783 first opened the skies to mankind, gained their buoyancy from hot air stoked by a brazier beneath the open neck – so on returning home I made a three-foot fire balloon tailored with tissue-paper gores of red and white, edge-glued to form a sphere, and set a wire frame across the open bottom to hold a pad of cotton wool saturated with methylated spirits. We lit it. The envelope swelled taut and sailed into the sky while we watched spellbound.

To-day only a millionaire could afford a hydrogen-filled balloon costing some £10,000 to purchase and £300 for each day's flying, so it is back to the hot-air balloon at a third of the price, using modern constructional materials and techniques, and employing bottled propane as a compact, easily regulated method of heating at £10 for two hours of dream smooth floating.

I waited with expectancy for my promised initiation – but the day dawned wet and gusty. The field seemed appallingly small, and was walled with trees and strewn with rippling canvas marquees and booths. By the time I arrived, my two young aeronauts had unloaded the balloon, basket, propane bottles, and primus-like heater from the trailer, and the striped red, white, and blue envelope had been extended full length on the soggy ground, securely pegged down with fabric bands. Steadily the wind increased. A call to the Met. Office offered no hope.

'We'd better pack up,' my friends said. 'Perhaps we can fix

your flight another day. We'll be touring around all summer, and later in the season should be back in Somerset.'

I thanked them. It was worth waiting.

This growing sport of ballooning has great attractions, and is even less expensive than running a modest sailing or motor yacht; nor do the pre- and post-flight drills need more time and muscle than getting such vessels under weigh or snugged down at moorings on return, though it cannot be done single-handed. I found that the neatly folded Terylene envelope takes two people to withdraw it from its bag and extend like a long sausage on the ground, and additional help is desirable to spread it flat to full circumference and hold down. As with balloons throughout the ages, a wicker-woven passenger car is used because of the shock-absorbing quality for protection in a rough landing, and to rig is tilted on its side and secured to the steel bridle wires that encircle the balloon – for nets are no longer used. The rip cord is positioned, and the rip panel in the crown of the balloon is checked. Onlookers and crew hold wide the fire-proof skirt that encircles the generous opening at the base of the pear-shaped envelope, and a small two-stroke fan is placed on the ground near the aperture. Then with a clatter the engine drives in a torrent of air, and the great envelope begins to rise monstrously and swell. The skipper fires the propane jet, aiming the roaring flame cautiously through the skirted aperture. The envelope rustles and wrinkles. The heat is evident. The gaudy creature raises a bulging shoulder and slowly stands upright, swaying gently. With little bursts of flame the envelope is kept full, and the crash-helmeted crew step over the plaited rim into the basket.

The leaves were scarcely ruffling in the gentlest of breezes. The canopy of sky was silvered cloudless blue. With a modern hot-air balloon there is none of that difficult business of olden time when the buoyancy of a gas balloon had to be carefully weighted with sand-bags to hold it down and a handful released to get airborne. Instead a wave. The helpers stand clear. A primus-like roar leaps a hundred times intensified from the burner; there is a slight dynamic plucking, and magically the helpers' heads sink level with the basket rim, then disappear, and the ground is dropping away.

Swiftly above the tree-tops, higher and higher lifts the balloon, with ever extending vista of fields and hedgerows angled with sunlight throwing long early morning shadows behind the trees. The fragrant earth, so fresh and glorious, seems strangely still to those conditioned by an aeroplane's swift flight. The roar of the burner is cut, and in the startling silence a blackbird's song can be distinguished.

On the slow tide of the unfelt breeze the familiar landscape of Dorset drifts beneath the basket. Every secret is revealed, for the downward view is matchless. Only a helicopter offers similar stance. Many a time I have hovered with one to study the earth signs of ancient man; but it is a noisy, vibrating vehicle, and a large part of the pilot's attention is engaged in the manoeuvre of flying and snatching glances at the array of instrument readings, for engine failure at low altitude means a certain crash because there is no time to regain normal speed of gliding flight. Yet in the windless calm of a balloon basket all is repose, the flow of time unconstrained except for that sudden shattering primus-blast of the heater at irregular intervals to check descent and renew altitude.

Already a quarter of an hour has gone, yet glancing back along the aerial path the balloon has sailed, there, little more than a mile away, is the field from which the flight was started. That small distance cannot measure the magic of the experience. Look up, and the interior of the balloon spreads like the dome of a great cathedral. Peer vertically down over the wicker rim of the basket, and there is no sense of height – only the green turf unrolling beneath, the slow passage of trees, each branch and glittering leaf so individually clear that it reveals the ease with which a bird recognizes its territorial nesting place. Even the cruising passage of butterflies can be watched with a flash of understanding of their purpose. Gaze obliquely through any quadrant of the compass: everywhere the mark of man, his

47

footprints enshrined by footpaths and winding lanes, the sign of his hand imprinted on field and hedgerow, the chequer-board of woods and fields reflecting the unrecorded story of ancient struggles, victories, regrets, loneliness, happiness.

Implacably the great balloon drifts onward, drawing its rounded shadow slowly across the present and the past. On one side is the ridge of the Dorset heights; on the other lies the Blackmoor Vale, spreading far towards Somerset and Wiltshire. An hour goes by, and almost another. The sky is limpid as a mill-stream; a dreamlike calm lies serenely across the countryside, the land spreading into silvery distance as though one sailed the mists of time. But every now and again the vision is abruptly fractured when the skipper gives that sudden startling burst of primus power.

He is looking at his map. Almost twenty miles have been traversed, and the bottled propane will soon be down to the reserve. He has spotted a large flat field in an area of few trees about a mile away.

'Seems O.K.,' he says.

There is an air of anticipation as the balloon begins to sink. The crew tighten their crash helmets.

The skipper nods approvingly. 'It's going to be quite easy in this gentle wind, just keep your legs slightly flexed, and hang on until we settle.'

Nevertheless landing can be a tricky business, for the rate of descent must be accurately gauged and checked with bursts from the heater. Watch must be kept on telephone wires, electrical cables and pylons, trees, hedges, buildings, and even cattle. If the horizontal speed is excessive it can be a very uncomfortable occasion, for the basket and its crew would tip over sideways, bumping heavily across the ground, dragged by the wind in the partly deflated envelope.

But to-day it is under expert control, and the mild breeze offers no problems. Gently the balloon descends, dropping at five feet a second but readily arrested by a well-timed burst of heat. All eyes are on the field which seems rising towards the crew rather than giving any sense of the balloon descending. The horizon grows circumscribed; vanishes. There is only a diminishing acreage of grass. Slowly, slowly the meadow lifts nearer. At forty feet comes another startling roar from the burner; the balloon seems to poise, lowers itself, and gently touches. There is a moment of silence as the cooling envelope begins to subside. There was no need to pull the red emergency rope which detaches the panel in the top fabric to allow hot air to gush out had the balloon become the wind's plaything.

'Now we just wait,' said the skipper as he watched the slowly capsizing, gaudily striped fabric as it cooled and emptied and flopped to the ground.

How different this calm, thistle-down landing from the account which long ago my friend, that pioneer woman balloonist Gertrude Bacon, gave of her experience as a young girl at the end of the 19th century when she, her parson father, and professional balloonist Percival Spencer lifted from Newbury at four in the dark of a November morning in their coal-gas filled balloon and sailed away due west above an unbroken strata of high cloud; then as the day grew warmer, lifted uncontrollably still higher. With a hot-air balloon, altitude is regulated easily with the burner, but Spencer's gas-balloon had no means of reducing buoyancy nor checking descent other than gradually emptying the unhandy ballast of numerous small sand-bags. However, after several hours they began to descend, and in mid afternoon, the sun's heat lost, dropped through the last low clouds to discover an unexpectedly storm-wracked land just below.

The adventurous Miss Bacon in later years recalled: 'Spencer ripped the emergency panel valve and we sank almost sheer upon a favourable spot, but we had not reckoned on so severe a gale, for it swept our half empty silk balloon over the ground with the basket bounding in great leaps behind it. Then crash and crash again! And we, all in a heap, clinging to the ropes as the car ploughed forward on its side. The pace was killing. We crashed through a barbed wire fence. An oak tree was approaching right in the way. With another crash we were into its top which was entirely carried away in our rigging and plumped down in the next field – but in the root of the tree our anchor, futilely following, at last got a grip, and now our moored and dying silk was beating innumerable little holes into itself on the gorse bushes fringing a deep ravine.

'Breathless we scrambled forth. "The roughest landing I have ever known!" panted Spencer. "Ten hours aloft!" cried my dishevelled father, whose clothes were torn. "You were going straight for the sea and it's only a mile and a half away!" called one of the crowd which had gathered. But for the only time in my life I was fainting, for my arm had been broken.'

What is this lure of flying? The pleasure of the experience outweighs all else when we are participating, whether airborne by balloon, bird-like wings, or whirling rotors. The mode of flight is a matter of personal predilection and expediency. All have their appeal, though I prefer the aeroplane to the helicopter and the sailplane with its animated sense of response compared to the static serenity of a floating balloon – but each reveals a freedom that loosens the bonds of time, for the sky world crystallizes life's experiences, brings it into consonance, defines and elucidates man and his aspirations.

For the moment I may seem earthbound, content to repose on the terrace of my cottage, basking in the sun, listening to the song of birds, watching the wind play across the woodland trees. And then I hear the mewling cry of the buzzards soaring the summer breeze on tip-tilted steady wings, and know that soon, perhaps to-morrow, certainly on the next bright day, I must take to the skies again and watch the world from this airy stance, inbred with the spirit of all living things.

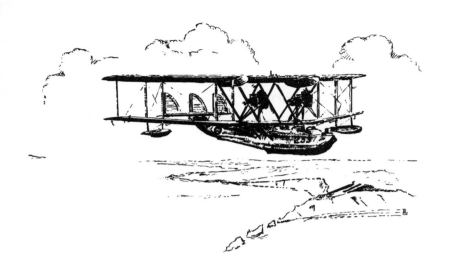

6 Quiet Interlude

On the first of the ebb we drifted from Woodbridge quay, heading down the ebbing Deben with sails listless in the clear Suffolk sunlight. All seemed unchanged. Beneath a sky of towering blue, in which a few gleaming cumulus floated becalmed, a quietude held possession among the meadows, heathland, and gently sloping woods. The gulls flew high, a host of birds sang far across the land, and close inshore a heron launched onto the air with slowly beating wings.

When nearby Martlesham Heath was the great testing centre for Britain's aircraft I knew this waterway well – but to-day was to return more than thirty years later, and the great, rough, heath-covered aerodrome of happy memory had long lain derelict. Now it had become the site of an expansion town, the echoing hangars pulled down, and memory of its adventuring men, and the hundreds of prototypes they flew, gone like the golden gorse and the whispering pines and firs. Often when

51

flying was finished I would walk from Martlesham village along the creek until I came to the Deben. There I would sit in the quiet, watching the ebb slowly expose the mudbanks and dwindle to a trickle. It was a place of silence except for the rippling call of waders, the harsh *kronk* of a heron, and the chatter of martins and swallows. My bible was the *Rubaiyat of Omar Khayyam*, and I might think of Edward Fitzgerald sailing these waters, imagining his cutter *Scandal*, with great club-topsail set, stealing along the river shore while the tall, untidy but dignified 47-year-old poet-philosopher talked deep mysteries and paradoxes to his red-headed, melancholy, tender-hearted but inarticulate yacht-hand 'Posh' Fletcher – 'a gentleman of Nature's grandest type,' his master wrote.

Fitzgerald had a ready eye for scenery, and loved bold colours, whether carpets and curtains, flowers, butterflies, birds, or the riverside arable crops 'as they grow green, yellow, russet and are finally carried away in the red and blue waggons drawn by sorrel horses'. He would rail against 'the petty race of Squires who only use the land for an investment: cut down every tree: level every violet bank: and make the country of my youth hideous to me in my decline. There are few birds to be heard because fewer trees to resort to. So I go to the water, where friends are not buried, nor pathways stopt up, and all is as at Creation's dawn. I am happiest going in my little boat round the coast to Aldbro, with some bottled Porter, some bread and cheese, and some good rough soul, like Posh, who works the boat and chews his tobacco in peace.'

Sailing the same course Fitzgerald would have taken down the sparsely marked channel, tide-rode, scarcely with steerage way, our boat of its own volition followed the perches, until on passing Martlesham Creek a light breeze caught the sails, and we headed for Methersgate quay on a straight reach; then curving with the channel starboard we saw the tower of Waldringfield Church and a line of anchored yachts close to the sandy shore of the right bank. I wondered whether the adjacent *Maybush* was still the popular inn it used to be after a day of sailing. Near by was the old boat-building shed where the sistership of my graceful pre-war racing 22-square metre *Tinkerbell* was built.

'Steer between the moorings and keep clear of the buoys,' I told the Mate. 'A great bank of shingle called a "horse" uncovers here at half tide. If you look over there you'll see the ripple across it.' I did not mention that on occasion I had stuck hard. It may be a long wait before the tide returns, but as compensation a dinghy can be launched and it is very easy to row across to Waldringfield. But we safely negotiated the obstruction, and beyond it the left bank stretched towards Shottisham Woods and then ran clear to the sandy beach of Ramsholt sheltering beneath a low hillside crowned with firs. Above the old barge dock stood the sequestered *Ramsholt Arms* where many a former river trip had been pleasantly delayed while waiting for tide to turn.

After passing the little dock and the dinghies parked on the hard, the zephyrs which had barely filled our sail strengthened sufficiently to ruffle the waters and make them alive. As we slipped down river, the water chuckling at our bows, there were more and more yachts at anchor, and three came over the tide under sail. On the opposite shore Kirton Creek drifted past, and behind it lay a countryside of quintessential Suffolk, calm and flat and seemingly eternal.

With a freshening breeze we sailed onward. Radio towers marking our destination came in sight above a long, low-wooded shore. We had been voyaging so slowly that almost two hours had gone, and though at high tide all this waterway would be a wide lake-like stretch, it now revealed only a glittering muddy fringe; but the channel was deep enough for a much larger yacht than ours despite the next big horse shoal in the middle of the river. We skirted the bank of the Felixstowe side, and found the anchorage full of motor-boats and sailing yachts. From the wooden pier a more modern ferry-boat than I used to know began to move towards the opposite shore and its cluster of houses and naval buildings. We turned across the ebb, saw the treacherous sandbank at the mouth, and with the last of our momentum drifted gently to the beach.

'On the other side of this rise there used to be some flying-boats hulls in a muddy little creek,' I said. But that was many years ago. They could not still be there: yet I felt strong prompting to look. We stepped ashore, pulled up the dinghy, and hopefully made for the road at the top where the same tatty wooden houses of old still stood, though a few newer ones had been added. We felt as though we were walking into the past, so little had it altered. The head of the creek was hidden a hundred yards further down the road. It seemed impossible that we would find, moored among crude houseboats and dinghies or resting on the mud, those seven or eight ancient wooden flying-boat hulls which long, long ago had been dumped from the R.A.F. marine testing station hard by Felixstowe docks in the estuary mouth of the River Orwell. Several had been rotting F.3 and F.5 relics from the Great War, and two or three had been converted into houseboats; another was said to be the Felixstowe Fury triplane; and there was at least one beautiful boat-built hull which I thought was the Fairey Atalanta. With diminishing expectation we walked along the road and found the saltings. At first glance there seemed to be only the same old derelict fishing boats surmounted by crude cabins. As they at least represented boat-building antiquity I made my way across the tussocky mud to study their maritime archaeological interest.

'Look!' cried the Mate, cautiously sliding round the stern of a hundred-year-old hulk. And there, resting on the weedy mud fifty yards away, was the old-time hull of a flying-boat which every R.A.F. mariner pilot regarded with affection – a wooden-planked Supermarine Southampton, its varnished, yacht-like finish long lost beneath drab, dirty grey paint, and the top decking fitted with a landsman's 'lantern' roof of glass to give standing room so that it could be used as a houseboat. Even her chined planing bottom seemed almost undamaged, and the original metal fittings were still on her stern.

'What a find!' I said.

'What will the R.A.F. Museum think of that!' exclaimed my companion.

My thoughts raced far down the years to a day in 1927 when I visited the Supermarine Aviation Works at Hythe on the shores of Southampton Water, hard by the ferry that ran across the commercialized River Itchen. On the narrow hard outside the little factory it was with excitement that I saw, what was for me, a glamorous sight – a large and beautiful biplane flying-boat with rounded wing-tips, twin engines mounted midway in the vee of widespread centre-section struts, and a varnished wooden hull of glorious workmanship which swept upward at the stern to carry a large monoplane tail surmounted by triple fins and rudders. Though I had heard of her, I had never before seen this latest acquisition of the R.A.F. – the Southampton, powered by two of the 450 h.p. Napier Lions which at that time had swept the skies as the ultimate in water-cooled engine design.

Devised initially as a civil flying-boat by Reggie Mitchell when he was only twenty-nine, this Service version established Supermarine with their first big production orders. Its glowing hull had been moulded by boatbuilders of highest skill, using narrow carvel mahogany planks on slender frames and stringers of rock-elm secured with thousand upon thousand copper rivets. Beneath the circular sectioned hull the broad, stepped planing bottom was painted white like a yacht. Complex though this beautiful flying-boat seemed, the prototype had been designed and built in a mere seven and a half months, and it was an ideal performer from the first, with clean sea behaviour, easy handling whether on water or in the air, and, unlike all previous flying-boats, had airborne ability to turn with ease against the live engine when the other was switched off.

'Would you like a trip?' said Henri Biard, their chief pilot – a youthful hero who had attained early fame when he won the Schneider Trophy at Naples in 1922 with a little racing biplane

55

flying-boat Mitchell had designed; though it had been soon superseded by the daringly aerodynamically clean twin-float cantilever monoplane S.4, and was being followed by that shape of the future, the S.5, which, all unbeknown, would presently lead to the Spitfire as the crucial fighter of the Second World War.

'Would I like a flight? You bet I would!'

'Up the ladder then, and into the second cockpit.'

The machine was facing the turbid water of the Itchen, resting on a special beaching chassis which could be quickly discarded when the machine was afloat at the bottom of the slipway. It seemed an enormous climb to reach that cockpit. I found it had duplicated control, with car-like steering wheel on the elevator column to operate the ailerons. The wide hull made the space within seem enormous, though I thought the tips of the propellers each side were perilously near.

Biard was separated from me only by a narrow strip of coaming. 'Here's a helmet. Clip in the speaking-tubes,' he said. With their aid I could hear the engine-starting procedure, resulting in a shake and roar and rattle as the port engine fired – quickly followed by the starboard. Presently first one and then the other was tested at full belt. The blurred propellers slowed to whispering semaphores, and the machine trundled down the slipway, restrained by a team holding ropes. A pause while a man with long thigh boots withdrew the pins of the beaching chassis – and we were away, motor-boating past the industrial buildings of the shore-line to attain a windward run where Southampton Water opened wider.

'Off we go!' shouted Biard.

The roar of engines enfolded me. There was rasp of water; gale of wind; the hull bumping through little waves. Heady with adventure, I hardly felt the boat change trim as she gathered speed, but there came a glorious skimming and lifting, and a cascade of water plumed on either side almost touching the wings. A turbulent trail of bubbling eddies reached down Southampton Water, and an ever spreading vee of waves was drawn from her keel. I saw, rather than felt, the control wheel come suddenly back. With a last rasp and jolt the Southampton lowered her tail and trusted her wings fully to the air. The sea and the sky! The uplift and strength of water; the smooth, icy support of the air! Each moment my fleeting impressions raced into extinction. This was perfection – a dream come true! The sun burnished the waters, pouring a golden luminosity which draped the far high downs in a warm glow, half mist, half lustre, that matched my youthful thoughts.

I was a tyro then, a new explorer into the unknown: this flight above the glittering inland seas of Spithead and the Solent, with the diamond shape of the Wight in unfamiliar guise beneath the bows, and the calm southern shore of England spread wide beneath the whirling propeller either side, was not merely a new experience but a re-birth into a different dimension of space and light that transcended my earlier passenger flights because this was the first time that I had fully comprehended the dominating vastness of the vista of water which can be seen from the air. The varnished wooden cocoon in which I sat behind the leather helmeted head of Biard had become the safely solid reality from which I saw the earth as a distant planet, where I remembered there must be people, not empti-ness, and that it was a world not of calmness, but of passions and perils as well as delights. I was torn between an arrogant sense of omnipotence and deep humility. I felt at one with the elements, integrated with the beauty and hazards of the sky.

I became aware of the engines being opened fully. Their carefully synchronized beat had changed to a dissonant *wong-a-wong*. Biard was making a level speed run, scribbling figures on his knee pad. I gulped the torrent of wind pouring round the little windscreen. The entire structure seemed to be leaning forward – straining. A tremoring vibration pulsed through the wooden hull. I was bitterly cold: deafened: no longer a god. Biard throttled, and turned his head re-assuringly.

'O.K. Finished,' he said.

We came gliding down in a long, whistling curve, engines

rumbling, the slipstream gentle. I watched the vanishing coasts with a pang for their passing and the end of the flight. The land lifted and closed in. I saw white yachts sleeping on the Hamble river, a dark coaster steaming up Southampton Water, and the port of Southampton itself, grey-blue beneath a veil of smoke. We began slanting more deliberately down, aiming leeward of the Itchen mouth. Wider, closer, spread the water: the shorelines became a narrow ribbon streaming past each wing-tip. Skimming: skimming: the rasp of water: plume of spray: the sudden retardation of buoyancy and arrested motion. Biard seemed almost casually turning the Southampton with one partially opened engine, and taxi-ing back towards the factory slipway as though no miracle had happened.

I thanked him as we stepped ashore from the motor-boat whose crew had moored us.

'That's all right,' he said with a kind of quizzical amusement. 'Maybe one day you'll take me for a flight.'

But I never did – and the last I heard of Henri Biard was that he had descended from the heavens to become the owner of a pub where many an old-timer met to yarn of what they considered were the golden years of flying.

All that was long ago, but to-day was filled with the echo of such thoughts. Somehow we must ensure that this Suffolk relic of those happy years should find a last safe haven in the R.A.F. Museum. It was a long business. Incredibly the Ministry of Defence seemed uninterested. They said they had no funds to buy the hull from the fisherman who owned it as a store for gear. Would any other country anywhere, possessing the world's last wooden flying-boat, propose to let it lie and rot? But for the skill with which one of the historian enthusiasts pulled strings, it would still be there in the mud. Months and months went by, more than a year, but presently the fisherman was supplied with an obsolete naval cutter in exchange – and by strange coincidence a huge R.A.F. trailer vehicle lost its way and came to Felixstowe only to find its passage barred by the Deben. Somehow that Southampton hull was hauled aboard. It now rests in the Museum store and perhaps one day will be given wings again so that other generations can reflect on the strange and thrilling creations of wood and fabric which young men so happily flew in the course of what they believed was their duty to a once glorious and spirited Empire.

7 Soliloquy with a Gull

The telephone rang. It was Ted. I had not seen him since the days when I owned *Airymouse* and housed her at the little flying club he had helped to establish on the unfrequented downland top of Compton Abbas before it became a well-known airstrip.

'I've something to show you,' he said conspiratorially. 'You'll like it. Could you meet me on Saturday at the old naval airfield at Henstridge?'

'What is it?' I asked.

A pause and a chuckle, '"Wot" is right,' he said.

And when Saturday came I found the answer. Waiting on the tarmac with an expectant air was a small white biplane of dainty archaic form almost identical with that earlier playmate of mine, the scarlet and black *Airymouse*.

'See!' said Ted, pointing to the name *Que Mas?* elegantly painted on his aeroplane's nose cowling.

'What more?' I translated.

'Forgive the pun,' said Ted, 'but as her dear old designer, John Curry, named his prototype *The Wot* I couldn't resist it. You know the story? Everyone asked him *what* he was building. Anyhow she's a peach. Like to try her?'

Ted had spent two years constructing his up-dated version. Where mine was braced with crossed cables that sang arpeggios in the slipstream, stirred by vibrations from the original two-cylinder engine, his *Que Mas?* had lenticular drawn-steel rods specially made at what must have been enormous cost, and she was powered with a 65 h.p. inverted four-cylinder Walter engine, similar to *Tipsy's*, mounted in a neatly cowled nose.

I tightly tied down the ear flaps of my deer-stalker hat, stepped aboard, and fastened the shoulder strap harness. My 'Wot' had offered only a belt. I felt for the rudder bar and tried the brake toe-pedals of the scooter type wheels which Ted had fitted to the modified undercarriage. Mine had no brakes and only the simplest springing, so taxi-ing in a cross wind usually meant walking alongside and pushing her round while manipulating the throttle, and the free-run landing could need quick rudder work and a burst of engine to prevent a swing.

'You're getting *effete* with these brakes,' I called to Ted.

'Makes it a lot easier,' he said. 'Petrol is on. Switch off. Suck in.'

He had already dabbled at the carburettor flooding mechanism and gave the glittering walnut propeller a few heaves.

'Contact!'

'Contact.'

A quick swing on the blade and the engine leapt into action stirring a vibrant pulse into the airframe, endowing it with life that became part of my own. Soon the engine was warm, was run to full r.p.m., responded tactfully to the switches, and died to a flailing murmur as I waved away the chocks.

She strained gently forward under a touch of power, and we moved to the runway, taxi-ing accurately at a touch of each independent brake. I turned her into wind after glancing around to see all was clear, then with wide open throttle rushed tail high, gathering the breeze under her skimming wings, and on tip-toe leapt into the sky.

Into the quiet clear sky of spring we climbed. Though it was now three years since I had parted with *Airymouse* her every characteristic was latent in this more powerful, faster relation, so I flew with a sense of long familiarity as we gently soared across the steadily widening vista.

Time was forgotten as I drifted over the sunlit fields and copses. What I saw was a vision of England, her very essence, with no impression that all this land was private property owned by many different men. Instead it was my England, that England for whom my friends, and many a man before, had died in the belief that it was to keep their homeland inviolate from any alien race.

Outside the windscreen the slipstream was a gale, but I sat loitering in a gentle breeze, for there is special pleasure in flying open-cockpit aeroplanes that no cabin enclosure allows: nothing but this physical contact of flowing air can give the impress of reality experienced by the birds. In a cabin one is insulated, shut away, viewing the vista of land and sky as though looking at a glass-covered picture in an aluminium frame; but with 'head-in-air' one peers through an exhilarating torrent of wind, sensing the slightest change of flow, feeling the warning decrease of pressure as speed is reduced, or the lurch of side-slip and yaw in turbulence; above all, the view is perfect, the colours and texture undisguised, as if looking at the world from a mighty hilltop, but with ever renewed interest because the panorama changes every minute.

My chief delight in flying has always been the vista that it gives – not merely the broad picture of the countryside and interrelation of each object with another, but the special view-point of its history; the traces of life of earlier men, the glimmer of their pathways, the faintly engraved marks of their lost villages, mystic stone circles, great ramparted fortresses on ancient downlands and high promontories, and the coastline of pre-history which can be seen beneath the water far off-shore at low spring tides of an unruffled sea.

In quiet contemplation I had been slowly climbing *Que Mas?*, until from 1,500 feet I could see the English Channel glittering beyond the Dorset heights, and away to the east the far white cliffs of the Isle of Wight rose from the water like the prow of a distant ship. I leaned from the open cockpit to peer obliquely across the lower wing at the multi-vallum outlines of the big Iron Age fortress crowning Hambledon Hill, on whose steep sides General Wolfe once marched his men in an excercise they would remember at Quebec. On the opposite side of the Hill was the last of a yew forest planted in the first Elizabeth's time to make the trusty long-bows of England. High above that straggling dark patch, a soaring gull materialized fifty feet below me, heading towards the distant sea, his pale grey wings held flexibly outstretched as he soared serenely across the landscape.

The quietly cruising bird looked up unflurried at my passing din – and I looked down and watched his easy soaring, recognizing that we mutually accepted each other as fellow voyagers with equal right to use the spacious sky. Maybe he was the ten-thousandth solitary gull I had met in many flights, discounting the thousands I had seen whirling above the countryside in squadrons or sailing the sea-cliffs in procession. All were vivid personalities – but so were the high-flying buzzards, kestrels, swifts, swallows, rooks, geese and wildfowl I encountered over the years. Even much smaller low-flying birds can be spotted and identified as they skim across the fields. The golden-green of a yaffle, the twinkling black and white of a magpie, or the chevroned wings of a pigeon are easy to distinguish when seen from a slow, moderately low-flying aeroplane.

Viewed from above, the beat of a bird's wing does not detract from its colour pattern because, in contrast to the blur of movement when viewed laterally from the ground, the up and down action is indistinguishable from the mean position. At most, all that can be discerned is a slight forward sweep at each down-stroke and almost imperceptible indrawing for the up-stroke. Colour marks therefore appear stationary and clear cut, so evolution has given the top surface of bird wings distinguishing marks comparable with the unmistakable squadron recognition insignia of old-time R.A.F. aeroplanes.

There is a distinctive yellow edge of wing and tail on a greenfinch, white shoulder patches contrasting with blue-black wings for the hawfinch, broad gold lateral stripes for the goldfinch, green wing bars for a siskin, white patches for the chaffinch, and a white wing bar for the gaudy bullfinch. Every species of wildfowl has its distinctive 'speculum' of bright colour. 'Protective coloration' is non-existent in almost every flighting bird when seen from above, for the procession of changing earth-greens and browns below them makes too great a contrast for effective camouflage. Only when a bird perches and folds its wings is advantage taken of possible blending of plumage with the natural background of its selected terrestrial environment, and so it tends to rest where least visible. Aiding unobtrusiveness is the much more important facility of stillness. To move is to draw attention. Since flight is the epitome of movement, cautious top surface colours are unnecessary, and escape from danger lies in power and manoeuvrability of wing.

The very structure of a feather precludes true camouflage, for the latter requires dull surfaces to prevent reflection. But a bird's wing is lustrous. A gull's feather held against the light becomes translucent Vandyke brown; viewed edge on, the blue end of the spectrum band appears, but when light strikes obliquely a silver sheen is reflected instead. The beautiful iridescence of a magpie's purple-blue feather becomes sienna against the light, and edgeways is rusty black, but when light falls directly on it, the sheen becomes apparent, and from root to tip reveals graduated spectrum colours. The ornithological glowing range of feathers of every hue chiefly comes from their property of breaking up light in similar manner to a prism, for basic pigments are only four – black, brown, red, and yellow – so green, blue, and violet are due to combinations of pigment and feather structure. There is no white pigment, but the effect of whiteness is obtained similarly to frosted glass by repetitive breaking and refraction of light. Hammer the brightest feather to destroy its structure, and the apparent colour vanishes: blue becomes dull black or grey, green becomes yellow, the colour of its pigment.

But this white-bodied gull who was my companion in the summer sky of Dorset was the quintessence of beauty as he sailed the calm sky, occasionally giving a light pat to the air as he corrected trim or sank slightly in areas where the warm air was rising too gently. I made a slow left-hand circle and came to him again, keeping sixty yards away. There almost seemed a look of recognition in his calmly appraising eye. He made no deviation – just that half flap or two from time to time as he enhanced the weak thermals, his long soft wings sensing the light pressure of air with lazy touch as they delicately flexed and arched, flying with instinctive ease.

We both were living an identical experience: saw the same sky world; the same far vista of fields, trees, and lifting hills – nor in those moments did I interpret that sunlit landscape in terms of man for he was too remote to be remembered. To me it was a pattern of familiar signs and symbols that dismissed all need of maps, the course I flew determined by the orientation of the sun and an in-built sense of time. Even the southern glow of a misty day can be enough. But while my small aeroplane may skim across the country carefree as a bird, the fallibility of man flying monster airliners, through heights and weather imposs- ible for birds, has every need of elaborate artificial guidance to find a precise destination into which he must fit his heavy and complex aeroplane with such exactitude that by comparison nothing could be easier than a bird landing on a twig – for the penalty of bad misjudgment with an aeroplane is death; yet for a bird it is merely the necessity of stretching wings for another try made easy by the slow, helicopter-like approach and land- ing speed.

I looked at my gull soaring with such easy nonchalance. Half an hour earlier, when I took off from the weed-grown runway of Henstridge, I had seen two sailplanes released from their tugs above Melbury Down and watched them trying to hold height

– but gradually they lost altitude. Although the drag of their tapered long wings was even less than that of the graceful gull, the bird's much lighter wing loading, despite lower aspect ratio, gave slower sinking speed which was easily eliminated by the up-currents, except when it gave that light pat with its pinions. Slowly I flew past him again. He held course, confident, happy, beautiful – a creature utterly fitted to its environment. For five more minutes I kept him distant company, then opened up the engine, drew steadily ahead, and let the bird vanish into the limbo of my past while he flew onward into the future. The landscape spread wider as I climbed, revealing every detail from deep Devon into far Hampshire – and all across the southern horizon the sparkling sea spread far and wide and endless.

What is it that so enthralls in these great vistas? Is it the unfolding beauty, or is it an illusion of omnipotence, of being guardian to a toy-like world as I sit here in the heavens? Far and wide I see at a glance the result of men's long endeavour – a fair and beautiful land, but all too often blemished with industrial disfigurements. Life down there unfolds, unconscious of the eye watching from above, whether mine or a bird's. I gaze at this land of Englishmen with no sense of prying but with deep compassion, even with anguish that it is my possession for so small a time. I am an accident of chance, a whim of fate – but I fly on, still dreaming.

8 Threnody

Far away, in a land as big as Scotland, the jagged mountains of the Spitzbergen islands reared primeval icy fangs to a sun which at last held sufficient warmth to melt the snows on their southern flanks and valleys. Though a glittering plain of ice still lay unbroken upon the surrounding sea, hidden beneath a blizzard-swept white wilderness of snow that reached pathless for a thousand miles to the Pole itself, the northern spring was faintly stirring in the frozen ground. Already in the British Isles the pink-footed geese had felt the call and were heading, with restless flight, stage by stage towards those glacier-girded mountains guarding the secret places of their birth. Deserted and forgotten were their winter haunts by mudbank and salting of Severn, Wash, and Solway Firth. Northward and northward the great birds flew, diverting a little here and there, descending on the sea many times for rest and food – some setting course from island to island, from the Faroes to Iceland, Jan Mayen, Bear Island; others following the Arctic seaboard of Sweden and Lapland over the ice-packed waters of the North

Cape. Presently their whistling glide would bring them with glad trumpeting to the land of the blue fox and the white, the caribou, white bear, wolf and seal: Spitzbergen! The riven snow of the volcanic rocks would vanish in a few more weeks and give place to glowing mosses and red and white lichens. Minute trees, inches high, would burst into green leaf on slopes starred with red and yellow saxifrage and Arctic poppies. In company with eider-duck and kittiwake, skua and glaucous gull, the grey geese would find fulfilment with their mates, unaware and uncaring that from their happiness life would spring anew to repeat the ageless cycle.

But here in Somerset I flew misty skies above broad water-moors where miles of intersecting dykes, rhynes and ditches made silver edges, framing countless rectangles of broad pasture. Only a month earlier all this plain had been four feet beneath flood water spreading in lake after lake far across the land. Thousands of annually visiting wildfowl had taken possession, and from fringing stubble and potato fields, as my aeroplane swept past, small gaggles of geese would sometimes leap up on quick wings and speed away in a group. Watching them lilt into the hazy distance that hid the Severn shores I hoped they would fly beyond range of the occasional gunners whose punts could be easily spotted from the air, hiding in the cover of crimson-glowing withy plantations which pierced the mirror smoothness of the flood like bristling mats.

It is the white-fronted grey goose which comes in greatest number to this western area. They are found on the Severn's mudflats and saltings of December in gaggles and battalions many hundred strong, but by then the pink-footed species, which arrived in September, have vanished. Possibly those pink-feet which visit Somerset are transit birds still migrating southward – but, if so, their return route must be different, since they are rarely found on the water-moors during the rest of winter, nor do they re-join the emigrant white-fronts leaving in March, for both seek different destinations – the white-fronts to the Russian tundra and Artic archipelago of Novaya

Zemlya, while the pink-foots move more directly north to the volcanic sea-cliff ledges of Spitzbergen.

By the time that *Tipsy* carried me across the early skies of spring, the pink-footed geese were but a memory, for they had long gone. Already the white-fronts, in hordes a thousand strong, had started northward. Even as they left, others which had wintered further south-west took their place upon the Dumbles: but each day the numbers diminished, and now the last were gone. All over England their great wings had drawn wild music from the air as gaggle after gaggle, in long sequence, flew unseen across the skies of dawn, heading towards the colder seas of the lands that gave them birth.

In a great circle five miles wide my aeroplane hummed steadily round while a hundred thoughts and memories flicked through my subconscious. As I peered through the whipping slipstream at the familiar chequer-board of fields and dykes still slushy from the floods, I saw their grasses sere and bent, but I knew that by May the warming touch of spring would change the rich silting to lush grass, gleaming like emerald.

Throttling to slower speed we slid down the sighing wind. From far aloofness the countryside changed to such warm intimacy that I could smell the scent of earth. As the fields flung closer I rumbled the engine into life, and, as there were no houses near, skimmed low, leaping the brimming dykes until I saw a score of swans floating in quiet company upon an approaching rhyne. I pulled higher to prevent disturbing them. Their heads barely moved to watch our noisy transit. As *Tipsy* sailed past I could see that their carriage was more graceful than the stiffer, goose-like appearance of wilder swans. A glimpse of red bills bordered with knobbed black at their gold-tinged feather foreheads showed they were mutes, though what I hoped for was a black-tipped, yellow bill, bright as a sunflower, revealing a much rarer whooper or Bewick's.

Safely hidden though they were in the sheltered heart of the water-meadows from every prying eye, except another bird's or mine, they showed dazzling white from the sky when I looked at them from half a mile away. So dominant they were that I scarcely glanced at the half dozen drab but equally graceful immature birds in the midst of the group. Though their mottled feathers afforded no real disguise, they were comparatively inconspicuous because attention was diverted from them by the vivid contrast of their parents' snowy plumage. With such simple psychological tricks as this the wild guards young life. It is less restrictive than protective marks, because these require an unchanging background.

As the aeroplane returned towards the birds, one of those with duller hue took wing and held my eye, emphasizing that both clarity of colour and the deception of camouflage are entirely subservient to movement. The stationary swans became unimportant. With questioning interest, I followed the course of the ash-grey bird sweeping its wide wings like oars while it made a brief circuit before gliding back to the water. Wonder why it did that, I thought.

Swans and rhyne swept from sight to reveal a different strip of water empty of life when I swung the aeroplane round to seek the lone bird which had flown, conscious that its behaviour was untypical of a cygnet. For a day of misty calm the take-off had been phenomenally short compared with the usual laboured scrabbling aи d beating of a swan accelerating on a still water surface. And surely, when the bird was airborne the wing-beats had been too lithe and quick for a swan's measured, powerful thrusting? I banked *Tipsy* steeper, making the reflecting waters of the flooded dykes whirl glittering, and the subdued horizon of drowsing Somerset turned in a spinning wheel whose broad spokes were drab fields decorated with newly budding trees and hedges. As the swans once more swept into view, like white flakes scattered on a bar of silver, I checked my turn with touch of aileron and rudder, then slanted towards them. Even now they scarcely bothered, but a sudden swirl of water became a flailing bird, whipping the air with barred and mottled pinions as it lifted steeply from the menace of my wings. Over my shoulder, as the aeroplane went sailing on, I saw the grey bird complete an awkward little circuit, and slant into the water with a hurried splash.

Sharply I turned *Tipsy* to have another glimpse. Again the bird beat into the air, only to land at once. For a moment this puzzled me: then, with growing interest, I realized that what had been witnessed was the weary semblance of the wild rhythm of great goose wings!

A grey goose in Somerset as late in the year as this? I stared down, while my aeroplane circled wide above the birds. The swans were placid and still; but the water of the rhyne rippled in furrows where the grey bird thrust with powerful paddle stroke, and anxiously turned its head from left to right and back. It certainly was a goose. Fantastic! How could a goose be there, when the geese of our British winter already were back in the Arctic sea of their summer home more than a thousand miles away?

When geese on the ground are disturbed by a low-flying aeroplane, however small the noise, their instinctive action is to gain mobility by escaping into the untrammelled air before the machine is closer than half a mile. Yet those several sallies past the bird had caused it to rise only long enough for a half circuit across the bank, then land immediately, close to the spot it had left. After that it grew tired, and could do no more than swim with hunted urgency across the narrow stream when I flew past once more. It was then that I realized it had no marking of distinctive white upon the dusky forehead.

'That seems to be a pink-foot, not a white-fronted goose,' I muttered incredulously to *Tipsy*, for the pink-footed geese had left the shore mudflats at Christmas. Could this be a straggler from France or Spain which had lost its way on the long flight back to Spitzbergen? The mist-blue sky could give no answer except hurl back the clangour of my engine-driven flight.

Next day I flew again. Storm after storm hung shadowed beneath grey skies. Shafts of light poured between them, as though through the stained-glass windows of a great cathedral. Where rain fell in ragged veils the countryside grew indistinct

71

and presently was blotted out; but after each deluge slowly passed, the earth lay glistening and darkly naked. On the sodden water-moors, glassy pools quickly filled every hollow on their regimented squares.

As I dodged around the storm clouds I remembered the pink-foot, and slanted steeply down to the great rhyne of Aller where yesterday I had found the bird hidden in the untravelled vastness of the ditch-defended water-moor. There was no sign of him. Swans were still nearby, floating like white lillies on the unruffled water. A tall grey heron standing unobtrusively on the side of the dyke sprang into the air with startled tumble of wings – and then, with confidence restored, drifted leisurely away. Lapwings clouded up, twinkling black and white. Rooks, jackdaws, starlings, and a flight of teal rose dark against the sky. With characteristic wing-beat, each group circled round and away.

Skimming rhynes and ditches bordering one soaked meadow after another, I headed west across the moors. With light pressure on the controls I made a mile-long leap across a spur of rising ground on which stands the ancient monastery and stone cottages of King Arthur's Isle of Muchelney, and, dropping on the other side, flew low across North Moor to look for wildfowl among the new flood water that filled its withy beds and ditches. Almost at once I saw a punt lurking in a narrow clearing between two tall sets of withies, and, though the wildfowl hunting season had been closed these several weeks, I could see a gun lying in the stern. The men stared up and waved. Had I been a bird it would have been an easy shot to get me. A duck, winged in this manner, might alight or crash on any of the partly flooded areas I saw, and dropping steeply down, tortured and terrified as it sought the immediate yet illusory safety of the ground, might fall into a waterway hidden from the punt by the red withy thickets. Did that explain why the lone goose had refused to fly, although its kin had long since left in strong flighting gaggles for the north? Was it winged by shot? Almost certainly.

I turned back to search again for the pink-foot on the fifteen square miles of the Aller rhynes. Suddenly I saw it half a mile ahead, rising with slightly lagging stroke to make an unsteady circle before settling where sedges fringing the bank gave false hope of cover. The bird had swum or flown to the far northern side, and now was sheltering in a still narrower flooded ditch close to a high-banked river running across the head of the water-moor. Carried by that current, it would not be difficult to find other ditches eventually giving access to the next moor, and in turn to others lying like stepping-stones northward. I began to feel convinced that the bird had a wounded wing, and, with sustained flight impossible, was trying to migrate by navigating the maze of canal-like ditches, paddling slowly, perhaps painfully, ever north. As it struggled through the gradually warming English countryside, did misty memory fill the slow hours with thought of icy seas breaking against the beetling cliffs where Arctic breezes lifted uncountable geese on excited wings to seek fulfilment?

I would have liked to tell that day by day I followed the progress of the bird, ever northward by ditch and rhyne, brooklet and river, constantly moving towards the far land of its wild desire. In fact, I never saw those great grey-brown wings again. Yet time and again the long arm of coincidence rounds episodes with unexpectedness that in the end carries conviction of inevitability. So with my goose.

More than two months later I was at Weston Zoyland on the Bristol Channel side of the Somerset Moors. At the Inn they were telling of the flighting of duck and swan when winter gripped the land, and of occasional geese heard calling in the stillness of the night and sometimes seen by day.

'What kind of geese?' I asked.

'Gaggling grit ole birds,' they said.

'Any white-fronts?'

'Hunneds.'

'Any pink-feet?'

'Zumtimes.'

'Seen any since Christmas?'

'Aye.'

Maybe I looked surprised.

'Tell'ee zummat that'll make'ee think,' my informant added, winking broadly. 'Varmer shot un week or tü back – mebbe a month. Down tü Kings Rhyne. But 'ee were a präper scrawny little old bird.'

9 Will o' The Wisp

To mark my sixty-fifth birthday I made a sailplane flight.

I had not flown one for fifteen years, and it was longer still to the days when slender winged *Pegasus* used to bear me to unexploited skies. The nostalgic wraith of memory intermingled with the dust which lay thickly on this little sailplane resting in a cobwebbed barn. I hoped she slept quite unaware that never again would we sail the winds of heaven because war's neglect had made her bones grow old. Who dare whisper that other men and other wings had scaled the heights we knew and won them for their own, forgetting us?

No flights I ever made could give more pleasure than the silent soaring of my sailplane, as eagerly she pressed against the summer breeze reflected upward from a steeply sloping hill. An open cockpit brought all the perfume of the earth, and the wind on my face gave reality to flying. Many the hours I spent drifting to and fro above the unfrequented Dorset heights, watching soft cloud shadows skim the sunlit quietness of downland slopes. In the whispering silence of my flight I would see mist-softened vistas where oak and ash, elm and thorn outlined ten thousand drowsing fields won from the waiting wild by long generations of stubborn, freedom-loving Englishmen. Or it might be the Channel shore of beetling cliffs along which I soared, gazing far across the glitter of waves and white-topped crests to where infinities of sky and sea met in a pale-blue arc of emptiness. There were other times when I was a bird circling in the sunlight, canting this side and that, lifting and dropping and rising again with sure and joyous control and the exuberance of new discovery. Those quiet heights, cool and clear and fresh as wine, induced so strong a sense of consonance with all the beauty of the silent land that I saw it as a heritage which no man must destroy for his material gain. None could imagine that the world was on the brink of terrible disaster: all was serenity as I floated on the ice-smooth air.

A long time ago, those sunlit days – severed from now by the concussion of bombs, by the quick courage of those Immortal Few, by new aeroplanes, different faces, bells tolling for the brave, happiness and sorrow. When at last that war had ended, gone were the easy days; and in a world groping for new paths it was no longer expedient to soar with a sailplane the old skyways. No more those quiet places: only the thunder of swift aeroplanes could lift me now to the realms of escape. Fantastic power gave speed and climb so great that England diminished to a village, with France a city five minutes distant, and the storm-tossed Atlantic reduced to a rippled waterway crossed in four hours. Research and yet more research opened the portals to even more imaginative vistas and revealed the pathway to the planets and the mysteries of the universe.

When there was opportunity I still sailed my small yacht,

and the unhurrying sea gave seclusion from the fevered pageant men call progress. The wind's throb, and the smooth, unflagging lift and fall as the bows crunched through the water sometimes reminded me of the gull-like, engineless flight I used to enjoy. I would watch, with ghost of old longing, the sunlit wings of the sea birds serenely soaring the white cliffs of Dorset. It seemed that the great open expanse of the seas gave a different and more intimate sense of freedom than in the sun-white blaze of heights I achieved with powerful aeroplanes far above the filmy cloud-puffs veiling the world of men. The oceans spoke of the globe's genesis and continuity; the heights echoed the eternity which has gone and the shadow of endless aeons that will come. With both there was the peace that many seek – free from the brazen blare that is civilization's travesty of life. Yet always, when I descended from the heights, the unfolding world from which I had fled swiftly linked me once more with its intimacy and I felt profoundly happy to walk the earth again and be among its people.

But the magic of a softly sighing sailplane can be greater than the immensities disclosed by a high-flying aeroplane, for it has much the same direct communion with the elements as a sailing ship. In the summer sky, the tide sailed by my open-cockpit glider had been time itself, flowing with smooth continuity from the far world of yesterday to the almost visible coming of to-morrow. There was deep content in sailing the hilltops, beating to and fro, and sometimes lifting high on a bubble of rising air and setting course from one glowing cumulus to another. I seemed to be winging across seas of music, uplifted by the spirit's delight.

Though yachts, with their wind-inspired wings, had taken the place of my leisurely sky sailing, there were moments when I would sketch the slender wings and body of some new aerial creation which might one day be built to restore me to more silent skies than those of test flying. They were the Phoenix birds, arising from the ashes of old desire, born for an hour or two of speculative interest, then doomed to extinction.

But now at Compton Abbas a gliding school had recently been established. Discussion became spiced with cloud fancy and all the sunny jargon of flight sustained by the atmosphere's dynamic energy. Maybe I was Rip Van Winkle talking.

'You should try it again with these modern sailplanes,' urged the young instructor.

'Far too out of practice to risk those beautiful machines of yours.'

'Not to worry. You can try with me in our new two-seater.'

Thought raced down the years and I saw again the fair curves of the Dorset hills I used to soar. I remembered the long hours of tranquil flight and the steady breeze sweeping in from the seas, fragrant and heady. Gulls flew in procession with me, translucent wings pliant to the same currents and eddies that rocked my miniature sailplane. Swallows flashed blue fire as they flicked from turn to turn, and the dark plumage of wheeling rooks became silver glazed as they caught the summer sun. A score, a hundred, small birds flitted on bright wings from shrub to shrub or brushed along the grassy hillside, happy and unfettered, fulfilling life's purpose with undismayed instinct.

Yes, I mused, I'd like to lean upon the wind again and watch it all: the sea, the birds, the quietness of the earth. But what I said was: 'O.K. We'll have a go.'

He led me to a sailplane, remarkable for wings swept forward, sixty feet in span and four times the area of the light gull-like single-seater I used to fly so long ago. No wooden creation this, but ultra modern, with metal-skinned fuselage seating two in tandem enclosed with a Perpex hood that swept from wing to nose. Alas! the perfumed breeze all lost, I thought; ho more of that sharp, invigorating tang of sea, nor velvet pressure of the sun-warmed air as it flowed exuberantly upon one's face – no more! Such primitive delight had given place to competitive streamlining for maximum performance.

They held her level. I stepped into the front cockpit and the instructor took the rear.

'You've been aero-towed before?' he asked.

I nodded but did not say that it was years before he was born! A thin loop of wire cable was hitched to the nose of the glittering glider; the other end snaked down the runway to a Piper Tripacer waiting with engine running. A helper standing at our wing-tip signalled with a fluorescent bat.

The Tripacer began to move and tugged the gently swaying sailplane with gathering speed. Both machines rose smoothly into the air. I was pushing on the stick to hold the nose well down yet keep a little higher than the aeroplane. Steadily we rose, pulled by the silver thread of wire, the Tripacer flying on a long slow slant to 700 feet, then made a wide and steady turn while I tried to hold precise formation at fractionally greater radius to keep the towline taut. If the towed machine gets on the inside of a turn the reduced tension of the slackened line causes the sailplane to lose height and there is risk of à jerk when it is ruddered back into position, easily resulting in some hair-raising oscillations and maybe a quick release by the discomforted tug pilot. I was so engrossed with holding station that I was barely aware of the changing landscape – only of the Tripacer's wings etched like a cross-bar target against the blue and the necessity of holding the precise angle of our interconnecting wire.

'Comfortable, isn't she?' came the voice of the instructor, and I nodded as though she really was. But in fact the controls felt remarkably stiff due to the speed of tow, slow though it seemed to the *Tripacer* pilot.

Steadily we climbed. Maybe it took five minutes to reach 1,200 feet, but it seemed a lifetime. A few cumulus were scattered far across the sky.

'High enough. You can cast off now.'

I groped for the scarlet knob of the quick release. 'Right,' I said, and pulled.

The cable separated and trailed from the Tripacer like a sting. I let the sailplane lose her excess speed. She became alive beneath my touch. Like a boat lifting on the calm swell of the

ocean, slowly and regally she sailed the air. That this was a
miracle of floating with no loss of height, despite our thousand
pounds mass, was shown by the little green pip steadfastly
holding position in the variometer's capillary tube. As though
sighing with pleasure, the sailplane slid buoyantly along the
skyway of lifting air. Concentration relaxed; an old and happy
familiarity returned. Cautiously I looked back and saw the
great wings resting solidly and motionless upon the passing
wind. The metal-structured cockpit already was as familiar as
the Spitfire's of old, with the same illusionary impression of
indestructibility as we passed in silence and tranquillity high
above the waiting fields; but I felt she handled more like a
bomber than a fighter.

Time turned back to the sunshine of my yesterdays. It was
the old intoxication. We moved with serene slowness, curving
from one perfection to another despite the heavy rudder.
Minutes no longer rushed like a cataract, but flowed with
leisured movement so that we could gaze unhurried at unfolding vale and hill resting at peace beneath the wide calm sky.
This was a divine uplifting, a paradise, though I missed the
fragrant breeze. I stared around in delight.

'Red's showing,' urgently shouted my friend, and with
sudden dismay I looked at the forgotten variometer.

Two feet a second down! Inexorably we dropped, yet so
gently that the sailplane was sinking slower than a falling
feather. Circling first left and then right, I tried to find another
thermal. Thought of everything except piloting technique had
fled. Sitting tensely still, we watched alternate hesitations of the
green and red indicators, but always it ended in victory for the
red. Our initial height was halved. Down and down we went.
Soon a landing seemed imperative, but as a last hope I steered
for the blue ribbon of road edging one side of the landing strip,
hoping the springtime sun had heated its tarmac surface
sufficiently to make a thermal which would augment the
vagrant breeze on the downland slope. Almost at once the red
pip hid and the green rose fractionally. We lingered drifting

above the road, sometimes climbing slightly, but more often barely holding height.

'Don't get too far away,' advised my fellow pilot. 'They hate it if you forced-land with this trainer because it holds up instruction.'

At that moment the gods smiled – or if it was not their smile I saw, at least my eyes discerned over my left shoulder a sign. I turned wide towards it. My companion touched the dual controls as though to take command. Green and red danced erratically at the bottom of their tubes. I stared rigidly ahead and upward. As the seconds passed in safety I continued turning hopefully. The altimeter still read 500 feet, and the airfield was half a mile astern. But the green began to show. Half a foot a second climb presently increased to one and then two. Five hundred feet became 600. The vertical current strengthened and the climb became five feet a second. Trees grew dwarfed. The horizon stretched broader. We reached 1,000 feet still circling, 1,500, and presently almost 2,000. At ease we looked around the sky kingdom that had been restored to us. Everywhere a vast prospect of downland slopes and green fields, captured in a net of hedges, faded into hazy horizons. We sailed smoothly on, the warm wind singing gently around the cockpit enclosure.

'That was a lucky break,' my companion said. 'What made you do it?'

I shrugged my shoulders as nonchalantly as possible. Half a mile away, I could still see a glint of white as the gulls I had followed upward turned on effortless wings, soaring into the distance on the rising air as they journeyed southward in the fashion of their countless forefathers.

10 Sea Chanty

Serene as a swan she rested on the still waters of the River Crouch – a great white schooner. She was the biggest yacht I ever sailed, and her mainmast truck towered ninety feet high. The sweeping curves of her slender hull glowed in the last rays of the sinking sun. Her mirrored image in the silver water intensified her beauty with a repose that enfolded her with the quietness of evening. Even the gulls were silent.

I launched the dinghy and rowed across – diamond drops of water from my oars stringing rings of ripples as I passed. The schooner's hull loomed higher, its row of portholes burnished by the scarlet sun. I drew alongside the boarding ladder, secured the painter, and climbed aboard. Within the shadow of the deck-house, smoking lazily, was Frank, her owner.

'Lovely evening,' he said. 'The others have gone ashore.

Back soon. We crack off at dawn for Rotterdam. Have a drink?'

I turned in early, and did not hear the rest come back, but in the pale light of earliest morning the deck hand brought a cup of tea. 'Casting off in half an hour,' he warned.

A light breeze was blowing coldly when we trooped on deck. Waders and gulls wailed and cried and chuckled. The sun edged above the horizon and began to dispel the morning mist, revealing anchored yachts and the estuary glittering and widening far ahead.

'Up with the main,' called Frank. He and his skipper had already uncased the sails. We began to winch the huge Bermudian up its bronze track. The gaffsail on the fore followed.

'Now the staysail.' The white canvas rustled up and lightly began to shake, followed by the jib.

With a grind and rattle and splash the mooring was dropped. Like a drift of thistledown, like a feather floating on the wind, our ship, with all sail set, imperceptibly moved away as sheets were hauled. A ripple broke from her bows. There was a quiet hiss along her sides. Obedient to a touch on the wheel she threaded her way among the anchored yachts and presently left the last behind.

'What about breakfast?' said Frank. 'Skipper will take her out.' A whiff of steaming coffee and eggs and bacon was drifting through the open skylight. With appetites whipped by the fresh morning air, we trooped into the main cabin. Presently a rhythmic bounding revealed that the protection of the river mouth had gone and we were breasting the swell of the green North Sea. Why idle in this splendid cabin? I went to the cockpit. The whispering wind blew fair and true from north-east – almost perfect for our course. The ship heeled gently under the pull of sails curving up and up across the blue until they reached the mast trucks swaying endless circles as the hull reponded to the waves.

'Like to take her?' offered Frank.

She required no holding as she pressed against the sea,

responding to the lift and fall. She felt dynamic, a creation of tremendous power, a gigantic man-made porpoise cutting the sea with effortless ease, yielding thus far and no further, imbued with strength to carry us over the edge of the world if need be. It was an old enchantment – the green seas lifting humpbacked in row after row to the far horizon, their hollows dark, sunlight sheening their sides with texture of wrinkled green velvet shadowed with blue and laced with silver foam.

As with flying an aeroplane, man and the instrument became one in performance and mutual dependence. Lightly holding the big teak wheel, I could feel the straining wind in her sails; the solid press of the seas; the buoyancy, akin to the lift of an aeroplane's wing, which sustained her above the depths. She was willing and quietly obedient, yet I could sense the strength of her character and knew that if wind and seas grew great she would accept my command even if I drove her roaring under press of sail, lee rail hard down, the tumbled seas racing along her length. But to-day the crew lay sprawling on deck, basking in sunshine and the warmth of summer wind. The hours fled by. The deck hand appeared with stacks of sandwiches and a crate of beer.

'I'll take over,' said Frank. 'You join them.'

All that afternoon, with cushions at my back, I lazed upon the foredeck. The lifting and falling bowsprit beat lilting time across the great arc of the horizon. On, on, alone in the emptiness, lulled by the roar of water, the murmur of wind, thoughts soaring into the sunlit skies where so often I had flown. The sea and the sky, sky and sea – which would I choose if I was restricted to only one? I found no answer. Both spelt freedom; both gave solitude remote from earthly complexities. Yet was it really possible to close one's eyes and look away from realities and rules: to fly the skies with the world forgotten; climb a mountain into emptiness; listen to a master's music and dismiss the man; dream a poem and ignore the fact that men are plotting war? Can one banish the impact of avarice and cruelty; dismiss the chaos of murder, robbery, violence, unbridled sex and drugs? Can one ignore the cold, deliberate march of technology which treats life as though it was a brittle thing of glass and chemicals? Where is the tolerance, the affection, the mutuality?. . . And yet there are men and women whose hearts' abundance can lift us to the stars.

I stared across the sea. What lay below? What marine forest? What sunken ships? What bones? What different world? Though I might grope for deeper understanding, see the beauty, feel the peril, the mystery remained. I could only be certain that I was an integral part of it – part of the endless flow of time, the immensity, the pulse that we call life.

Presently I was awakened by Frank. 'Marvellous sailing,' he said. 'If the wind holds we should make it by midnight. Come and have a sundowner.'

When I came on deck after supper, it was night. The wind had lessened; the ship was whispering through a quieter sea. To those who might see her passing, she would seem a phantom, a dusky figure moving through lonely space – but I knew the reality of her inward being, could feel the slow heave as she lifted smoothly across the swell of waters swirling past. I listened to the voices of the stars, but though they could fix our exact position upon the highway of the sea, they blinked and winked through infinities of time with other messages I could not read, and left me insignificant. Here were six of us in this ship, sailing through the quietness of night, the seas a darkness stretching outward to an horizon which had closed upon us, lit only by the stars. The skipper's pipe was glowing at the wheel, illuminating his face momentarily as he puffed. The minutes brushed past like the drift of air on our faces and were lost astern, while the ship went on and on with undiminished purpose on her course of faith. And though the skipper was there to steer us, and we had charts and compass and the loom of lightships to show that all was well, each of us was travelling a path of our own, eternally secluded, with only the past to guide us, and memory, and hope.

Late that night we drew alongside the quay at the Hook of

Holland where Customs cleared us. Sails were furled; the motor started; and down the long fairway of the Maas we followed the lamp-lit line of buoys that would bring us to the yacht harbour in the crowded port of Rotterdam.

A week later, having flown to Kiel and back to Amsterdam, I returned to England by helicopter on a day of low cloud and pouring rain.

'No wonder they need pumps for their polders,' said my co-pilot. 'If it rains much more the whole place will be drowned!'

We lifted from the great complex of buildings and hangars at Schiphol and edged round the Ijsel Meer to reach the coast. Gabled houses and avenues of waterway drifted past, dimly visible. It was only slightly better than flying blind. The windscreen was a blur. I opened the side window and peered through the torrent of ice-cold rain. The last of the Haarlem Polder, scarcely distinguishable through spears of rain, drifted past, and we recognized the thin line of coast and a different obscurity which was the sea. I turned the helicopter parallel with the thread of land, for it would lead to the mouth of the Maas, and then we could leap-frog the low islands of the Scheld and follow the coast of Belgium to the familiar shores of Calais and head across the Straits of Dover to Lympne, near Folkestone. It would be an easier and safer route to follow, though longer, than a direct compass course to England over that dank and ugly brown North Sea which we were skirting. To fly across it would have needed concentrated watch on instruments to prevent unconscious change of path from level to slight angularity which in seconds would end in flying into the water. Sky and rain and sea seemed indistinguishable unless I glanced at the dark shadow of coastline beneath my window. Though we would still have to use the artificial horizon and turn indicator as a constant check, the veiled shore would be our safeguard, helping orientation, and offering the necessary few yards on which to alight should the engine fail or weather clamp to nil visibility.

A week ago that same North Sea had seemed to have no guile. It was sunlit green, rippled with glittering waves, and our splendid schooner had sailed on and on, confident that the hours would bring harbour, and the voyage a chosen end. To-day the sea was treachery, and the sky a barrier. There was no promise of safe arrival. The helicopter was a mechanical, vibrating, soulless creation depending on continuous piloting, for this one had no system of artificial stabilization. At every instant I must be alert to set those whirling, vibrating wings to auto-rotation and drop to a safe landing. It did not worry me: I was conditioned to it; but amid the weather hazard of to-day, the sea voyage of last week seemed so much more certain of its destiny. Yet there had been other days, in smaller ships, when the winds had torn the seas to anger and I had thought how much easier it was to ride the skies with wings!

The wind and the rain: the sea and the sky – these were my familiars amid the evaporation and condensation eternally interchanging from the play of pressures and their generated winds that control the sea, the land, and even life itself. The theory of their mechanism is familiar enough – but we were experiencing the physical reality; and it was devoid of any semblance of science, imprisoning the mind with incoherence except in knowledge that a steady course must be pursued to subjugate the perils of this encirclement of water above, around, and everywhere below. The helicopter was a vault of noise, of shudders and vibration, of suspense in unreal emptiness – and only the passing minutes on my watch told that we were drawing nearer England.

A glance at the compass. O.K. – but the coastline was veering away. That yellow-flecked, wind-ruffled grey below and on either side was the sea, and it would be a long ten minutes before we saw a tip of land that preceded our next jump over water before making land again, and then another jump, more land, a little stretch of sea – and presently West Flanders.

'Who'd be a birdman?' asked my companion. 'Like me to take over for a while?'

I relinquished the controls. He stared fixedly ahead. Rain, rain like an opaque curtain around us, with almost indistinguishable ruffled water everywhere below: the elemental forces of the world at their careless uncaring. We were locked in a mechanism, unthought of, unprotected, mattering nothing if we among the world's teeming millions found an end in the water beneath. Not that this worried us either. We were only concerned with getting to our destination. But I felt an affinity with those men of two thousand years ago who expressed their awe of the majesty and power of the sea and the wind: 'They that go down to the sea in ships, that do business in great waters; these see the works of the Lord, and His wonders in the deep. For He commandeth and raiseth the stormy wind, which lifteth up the waves thereof. They mount up to the Heavens, they go down again to the depth: they reel to and fro, and stagger like a drunken man, and are at their wits' end. They cry unto the Lord in their trouble, and He bringeth them out of their distresses. Then are they glad because they be quiet; so He bringeth them unto their desired haven. Of that, men would praise the Lord for His goodness, and for His wonderful works for the children of men.' Thus spoke the ancients who knew few mechanisms but were close to the earth and the elements; who watched with careful eye the scend of the sea, listened to the wind in the rigging, and gazed high above the swaying cordage to read the message of the sky and racing clouds. And yet that was a question of degree. To-day, such is faith in computers and calculation, man can ride through cosmic space, land upon the moon, and from vast remoteness make safe return. So what was all this thought of encompassment in rain?

'Ostend?' queried by friend, briefly pointing ahead. 'Much better visibility now. This seems the tail end of the storm.'

I took the controls again. Through the side window I could see the blur of a town and its rain-swept jumble of roofs and streets. Soon we were over the familiar harbour, its long entrance like two needles jutting into the sea; and there, in the inner harbour, were bright-painted fishing boats and trawlers, not far from the yacht club where I had moored a big yacht for the night.

Still low cloud: but now the long flat coastline was clearly distinguishable, leading into distances that would take us home. I watched cars speeding along the coastal road, saw a style of architecture readily distinguishable from that of England, gazed at flat fields, browsing cattle, the quietness of a countryside we labelled foreign yet was no different in essence from every homeland that men call their own. The rain stopped. The fields were drab and wet, crouching beneath the low, dull overcast. The sea was lifeless, empty.

'I remember this place when it was bristling with guns,' said my fellow pilot. 'And there's the mole of Dunkirk – there in the distance. Boy what a week! Troops all over those beaches, and queues wading into the water to the boats that took them to our ships moored half a mile off. Can't imagine how the Jerries didn't get the lot.'

I gazed down at the great sickle curve of yellow beach, empty, its story buried beneath the unruffled sand, the heroes forgotten. Dunkirk, under a light pall of smoke, slid into the past. Ahead, the horizon was visibly brighter. Clouds were thinning. Here and there the sun was filtering through. A quarter of an hour, and we were flying with dappled sunlight brightly patching a green sea that suddenly had become animated and beautiful. At Calais I swung the helicopter at right angles, and headed for the invisible shore of Britain. The rifts of blue sky became bigger as the last low clouds drifted past. The dwindling cliffs of Gris Nez vanished astern. There was nothing except rippled waves, rank after rank, and presently a merchantman, small as a toy, with white foam bursting around its bows, as it butted the seas.

'Quite a wind down there,' said my co-pilot. 'I'd rather be up here, wouldn't you?'

Our passage through the air had been remarkably smooth, for the big articulated blades, as they swung round and round, lifted and fell, absorbing the eddying bumps of wind. But that same gale, judging by the buffeting progress of yet another ship, was raising quite a sea. The cross-Channel ferry passengers could not be enjoying their ride.

Suddenly, there was England! One moment all had been water and sky: at the next, there was a glitter of white from friendly chalk. The cliffs lifted higher, grew near and firm and real. The clouds were high and few. The sun was shining on England's green and pleasant land.

'Home, home,' misquoted my friend, 'is the wanderer, home from the sea,' and he switched on his microphone to call Lympne for landing instructions.

11 Requiem for a Peregrine

Five hundred feet below *Que Mas*, as she purred through gentle skies, the cultivated fields of northern Hampshire barely disguised the ancient downlands they overlay. Despite thousands of years of sun and rain and frost and the ploughing of the last two centuries, pits and mounds and circles refused to be obliterated and showed as deeper coloured growth where Stone Age man had made his monuments and dug for flint. A few miles further, a shadowed mesh of intersecting lines marked the cultivated banks of later Celts whose agricultural system lasted a thousand years until the Saxons ravaged and destroyed their peace. Flighting like an arrow across these shadows of long ago was the long straight line of Caesar's Portway, fringed with the woodland strip of Caesar's Belt. The track sped eastward across secluded and beautiful heights, on a course that nearly two thousand years ago served the Romano-Britons journeying to and from their fine city of Calleva. Then as now it was a highway of peace rather than of war and marching legionaries.

The broad *agger* of its original stone-faced trackway, three times the width of most Roman roads, emphasized the importance of its link with Sarum, two days' jouneying westward. Even after the tribal Britons of chalk-hill fortress and forest lair had for some generations accepted the pleasures of ordered existence in splendid cities under Roman law, the peasants of the down-lands held to their Celtic tongue and farming tradition. From my aeroplane I looked down at the spidery trace of their cultivated fields on which at long intervals might be superimposed the faintly visible vestige of a grassy rectangle, outlining a long-gone Roman posting station or rest-house. Through their past and their present, and miraculously through my own days into the future, the Portway ran, straight and lasting – like the great motorways of to-day that are imposed by the more powerful will of the urban on contemporary rural scenes that are relics of ancient ways of living.

Immured in my sky world of drowsy engine noise and rushing slipstream, I gazed speculatively at the fair earth made fertile by the bondage of men. Time had smoothed the struggles of creation and left a tranquil scene of patterned fields, green woods, and sleeping downs. The great emptiness of the sunlit countryside emphasized its self-sufficiency and absorption in the growth of rooted life. Ahead, I could see through a faint veil of mist the hazy blue shape of Beacon Hill looming beyond the level downland of Seven Barrows where the young de Havilland of 1910 had first flown a pioneer pusher biplane of his own construction powered by an aero engine he had built. He had been a hero of my school-days and even later, so it was with a thrill of discovery that I had located his field when flying long ago. But just before I reached it that day, there had been another of life's little adventures as I flew across the same great wood-crowned hill above which *Que Mas* was flying now.

Rooks and pigeons had lifted from the trees and sailed away, leaving a solitary slatey-blue bird whose fierce, blunt head projected from wings that curved like a sickle from the powerful body. Unmistakably it was a tiercel peregrine, fearless and free as the winds that carried him. Square into the breeze he soared, exploiting the gentle up-draught from the steep slope below, in no way disturbed by the muttering engine and noisy slipstream of my flight. He merely gave the intruding aeroplane a passing glance. It is those dark eyes, compared with the yellow irides of baser hawks, which distinguish him as a noble bird in the sport of falconry.

His pitch was a hundred airy feet above the topmost trees. I saw him move forward and sweep into a curve as I eased into a gentle turn that took me away from the hill. When I re-discovered the peregrine he was a dark crescent sailing above the trees at double the height of his previous motionless soaring.

I circled slowly, keeping him in sight. Interspersed with soaring, he gave several bursts of rapid flapping, but gradually the intervals grew longer as he lifted higher. Soon he made a last pat and began soaring steadily without further propulsive movement, canting with magnificent assurance round and round in a broad right-handed circuit. A hundred feet below, I banked my aeroplane still steeper, turning in a bigger and faster circle outside his orbit. Sometimes he ignored the machine – at others gave a casual glance, then swept imperi-ously higher.

Wider and more diffused spread the landscape as bird and aeroplane circled in the pale sunshine. Eight hundred feet became nine, and in another two minutes were fifteen hundred. Once or twice the slanting light fell on the peregrine's tilting wings in such a manner that I saw them lustred with glowing blue; but generally his silhouette was darkly incisive against the pale sky, and boldly vital. Here was the haggard of the falconer, master of the air, certain of purpose, slayer of thousands of wild birds by skill and strength of wing. Yet his role has no special cruelty – nor loftier beauty than all nature. It is a game of chance, with death the penalty to whoever loses; for the hawk who too often misses his stoop dies from starvation, as surely as his victim is forfeit for too great an error in manoeuvring to

93

escape. Throughout the scale, life is held by a perilously fragile thread; but who takes thought when the race is hot-blooded and death throws no warning shadow?

Certainly the peregrine flew as though my intruding aeroplane concerned him not at all. Two hundred feet above me, he gradually extended his circles until they were ten times greater than the quick turning of his initial climb. My throttled speed was only slightly faster than the bird's, the indicator showing 40 m.p.h., but although he soared so buoyantly, no further height was being gained. Barely perceptible, a few ragged wisps of cloud grew from the diffused moisture, and floated, trapped by a temperature inversion, just above us. They showed that the upward drift of air ceased at that height and fanned into the horizontal movement of the wind, preventing higher soaring.

Aeroplane and hawk went sailing on, separated by the valley's width as I watched his easy soaring. Then I worked into position astern, and edged towards him. The peregrine's wings glowed momentarily as they changed angle and caught the sun. Down he went. Down plunged the aeroplane. He was drawing away – his wing wrists hunched to his head, pinion tips trailing sharply pointed behind his tail. It was the silhouette of the supersonic aeroplane so recently evolved by man, though nature has used it these many thousand years. Down, down went bird and man.

I opened the throttle. The life tremor of the aeroplane changed and grew harsher. Speed swept from 50 to 60, then to 80 m.p.h. Five seconds we held formation, diving at some thirty degrees to the horizon. Next moment the peregrine, with wings still at an acute Vee, shot violently up – inclining steeper and steeper, until the axis of his body was vertical. I found myself looking straight up his back at the filmy sky. He hung there, like a reversed three-pronged trident – wing-tips and tail pointing at the earth, the great hooked beak held savagely towards the horizon – then with a movement so quick that it defied vision, he flicked sideways and downwards, whirling without visible wing movement into another, steeper dive.

Impressed by the absolute power and knife-edge finesse the bird displayed, I smoothed back the elevator so that my aeroplane lifted its nose in emulation so high above the misty horizon that the cowling loomed stark against the emptiness of sky and the land dropped from sight. Up I went, a thousand feet above the diaphanous cloudlets, with speed tumbling towards the stall; but before the needle could reach its mark I pushed hard rudder so that we somersaulted sideways, just as the peregrine had done, and went tearing steeply towards the earth.

Though the tiercel vanished during this manoeuvre, he materialized once more as the aeroplane levelled. I chased after him. He zoomed two hundred feet, his body inclining until it reached vertical – then that sideways flick and another dive. But this time he continued down, sizzling to the treetops on almost closed wings. It seemed he must hurl himself right into the foliage. Instead, when catastrophe was imminent, the slatey wings suddenly spread full and the dive changed smoothly into level skimming. Just ahead of him three grey pigeons broke from the topmost branches on frenzied wings. The peregrine turned from them in a superb curve that took him over the valley and back to the wood.

As he neared the trees another hawk, duller but even bigger, rose from a topmost branch and swept towards him. I could imagine the melodious chuckling call given by the tiercel to his mate, the great falcon who had joined him. Side by side they towered into the sky, alternately soaring and flapping. When they were half a mile distant, and five hundred feet high, a wide deliberate semi-circle was made. Together they gathered speed, then nosed steeply for the wood. I watched the great birds until they vanished in the trees. The leaves closed about them and were still. Nothing moved. The green world lay quiet with ageless innocence. The sun's brightness emphasized the emptiness of sky. Wrapped in solitude I flew on, my wings drawing a swiftly passing shadow across the history of the earth.

To-day, more than a quarter century later, those wings of bird and man were ghosts, but in that swift re-living of those moments *Que Mas* had brought me over the smoothly rounded slope of Beacon Hill, below which seven turf-covered burial tumuli marked the rolling downland field where Geoffrey de Havilland first flew. I pulled back the throttle. The wires lowered their high song and whispered. The little aeroplane's white wings canted as we came curving down; then I straightened her, and we headed into wind across the trees. A moment later the wheels were rasping through the grass and she was settling down. I switched off the engine, and got out. The quiet sunlight illuminated a scene that had changed little from de Havilland's viewing in the century's first decade – and the great chieftains buried in those tumuli would have recognized the drowsy noonday silence on the hills where once eagles and hawks, such as my peregrine, rode the wind-swept sky and saw the same cloud shadows sailing the grass-clad slopes as did ancient man and Geoffrey de Havilland and you and I.

Silence and sun; starry little flowers half hidden in the close-cropped turf; the clean downland breeze; this quiet land waiting throughout the years, this land of England which generation after generation have worked for and fought for and loved: will it be the same if I can re-awaken in two thousand years when all natural resources have long been extinguished by the greed of to-day's uncaring men? If there are still people here, they will have reverted to the simplicities of those nearby Iron Age men who were interred that same span of years backward towards the dawn of history.

All changes, and is forgotten. Who remembers de Havilland's name, let alone his tenacity, his genius? So few – for the great firm that he founded was absorbed, like others, into anonymity. And yet in this downland field the essence of his achievement lingers still, and to prompt it there is now an inscribed stone where once his aircraft stood. Will future generations understand the romance, the thrill, the endeavour that makes this place the shrine where the beginning of a great chapter was written in the crumbling sands of time?

The peregrine too has had his day. When I first played with him in the skies, above this rolling land of Celt and Roman, there were known to be more than six hundred breeding pairs. Six years later, rendered infertile by pesticides on crops swallowed by their prey, there were less than seventy. To-day there seem none in southern England, and the eyrie I knew in a lone clump of trees high on the Berkshire Downs, not far from this field of de Havilland's, was one of the last to be abandoned. The wind and the sun, the great sky places and the partly poisoned earth remain – but 'Bahrám, that great Hunter . . . lies fast asleep.'

12 Fugue in Time

The dripping trees were stilled and mournful under a sullen sky as we drove to the airfield. Gone was the anticipation of a glorious sight-seeing flight across western France and thence to the Gironde which we had hoped to use as a signpost to reach the romantic southern lands of mediaeval cities and sunburnt plains through which we once had steered a splendid ship five hundred miles from England to that river and then three hundred miles along France's waterways to find the blue seas of the Mediterranean. When I talked to the Met. Officer he was far from hopeful.

'There's a widespread depression across western Europe. No chance of clearing for a couple of days. Local cloud is ten-tenths at eight hundred feet with occasional heavy rain.' He glanced at the synoptic chart. 'It's hard luck, for at present it seems clear over Spain and perhaps O.K. in the Gulf of Lions. I'll get you an actual from Marseilles.'

We waited while he telephoned. There was hope. Maybe I could fly over the top – a thing I usually avoid because I had experienced so many engine failures in earlier years. But this was a twin-engined Cessna which had been loaned to me, and with one engine cut and its propeller feathered it could even cruise at 150 m.p.h. at 12,000 feet still with ability to climb at 250 feet/minute. I argued to myself that modern engines, such as the Cessna's turbo-charged, fuel-injection 340 h.p. Continentals, are extremely reliable – and at the worst, retractable undercarriages enable a quick pull up in a belly landing, though it rather spoils the aeroplane. So I waited in some doubt, my caution warring with anxiety to stick to dates and times and plans. It was almost anticlimax when Marseilles confirmed they had brilliant sunshine all along the Côte d'Azur, and that there was clear sky above a layer of cloud which covered the rest of Europe. That meant we should not see the Channel Isles, nor wild Brittany, and the Bay of Biscay would be hidden beneath that floor of cloud. Bordeaux would remain a name with port and buildings lost to sight, and the fair lands of the Canal du Midi, with cities such as Carcassonne, would be a half-remembered dream.

We filed a flight plan and boarded the Cessna – a currently conventional executive low-winger capable of 270 m.p.h. The comfortable cabin for six seemed remarkably spacious, though it was almost disconcerting to realize that the wing area of two hundred square feet was no more than my lightly laden Widgeon of old, for the Cessna had a wing loading as great as the war-time Spitfire and a correspondingly fast touch down and landing run. I settled at the controls, warmed up the engines, called the Control Tower, and was given clearance to move.

As I taxied out, it began to rain. The runway became blurred. Who could believe that this path of streaming concrete led to sunshine, gold sands, and azure seas? Not I. Yet as soon as the engines started I had become part of the mechanism – a computer, the electronic urge, the instinct, the calculating brain. My gaze became riveted on the blind-flying instruments but aware of the runway streaming past as I opened the centrally mounted throttles with the palm of my hand, letting the machine hold by its own volition the attitude set by its tricycle undercarriage. It steered easily; yet subconsciously I was keyed to a possible engine cut, the violent resultant swing, and the action that would be instantly necessary. I kept the flaps shut. She runs, gathering strength. The needle of the A.S.I. steadily moves – 70, 80, 90. At 105 m.p.h., having traversed all of four hundred yards, I pulled back the stick. A minute just gives time to become confident in the machine before we are in cloud. From the corner of my eye I see the speed has settled exactly at the requisite 140 m.p.h. for best climb and angle. So instinctive is a pilot's action that I am almost unaware I have selected undercarriage up, for my eyes are fixed on the gyro instruments amid the grey-white opaqueness suffocating the Cessna, but as I hear nose and main wheels thump locked I dismiss that part of the piloting sequence from my mind. Next I must reduce power to 29 inches and 2,100 r.p.m.; automatic control will hold it constant, so I change tc right hand on the flying controls. Artificial horizon and directional indicator show we are correct on each axis, yet I can feel the machine make each slight surge despite the immobile needles. I dislike this blind flying – a remnant of distrust from early days when I tested, with tentative flights into the unknown of overcast and cumulus, some of the still unproved early blind-flying instruments; for I had to discover the technique by trial and error.

I glance at the steadily moving pointer of the Cessna's altimeter: 2,000 feet – and only a further minute had gone since we entered cloud! Wings lean on fog-like emptiness; steamy puffs shoot past the window; the three-bladed propellers have become a more evident blur; noise is immolating us into silent passivity. Suddenly the cloud grows lighter. Brightness momentarily bursts from above, then darkness. Next moment we have slanted from the topmost layer and find a dazzling snowfield far as eye can see, and the sun is a high white-hot hole bored into the blue. I turn on course, still climbing, and confirm departure to Control. There are six hundred miles to go, and we, a solitary speck in the emptiness, are heading hopefully south by thirty degrees east. On levelling at cruising altitude I estimate we can reach Marseilles in two and a half hours, yet we seem suspended motionless, the atmosphere calm as a mill pool. The others begin to talk. From time to time I nod agreement, but my thoughts are browsing amid invisible distances. Soon a drowsy silence reigns lulled by the droning roar, the smooth vibrations tremoring through the structure, the warmth of the sun pouring into the cabin; and all around and above the endless white cloud floor is a dome of burnished blue sky. My thoughts go drifting, drifting into the past to find the reason for this flight – this voyaging back to scenes where youth was at the helm with no thought of to-morrow.

What was it that I remembered? There were four of us, and we said: 'The time has come to be free,' meaning we would be quit of petty tyranny, and find the earthly paradise of which we dreamed. So we went down to the harbour, boarded our big yacht, and filled her with stores sufficient for many weeks. Her sails swelled in the morning breeze – and lo!, we were away! The ship curtseyed as she met the ocean, then danced over the waves, careless that we had no plan except escape – for this was youth, we had rebelled, and were seeking adventure beyond the horizon's rim, sailing the ardent wings of morning to find a new haven across the seas.

The ketch settled into her stride, and presently was alone in a world of sweeping water deeper blue than any sky. It was as though we sailed an ocean no man had ever traversed, guided not by chart and compass but the vision young men see. Ah! But the gods love youth, and care for happy fools. They filled our minds with glamour, showed us the wonder of the deep, made each moment prescient with revelation.

It was youth and sunlight and freedom never again attained.

As I look down the years it has an illusive, unreal quality – like the intangible memory of a dream that had seemed so clear and bright. All time was our possession then. Our lives seemed to stretch endlessly ahead, like the sparkling sea on which we sailed. Hour followed hour, the wind murmuring in canvas and cordage, water scrunching under fore-foot and whispering astern, while warm sun flooded from a springtime sky. Sometimes, in quiet voices, we talked; but mostly we sat in easy silence, empty of thought, yet almost believing we understood the very secret of the universe.

The fair breeze held. The waves grew longer, the sea a richer blue, and the ship lengthened her step to match the Atlantic swell. When for the fourth time the sun sank, huge and round into a fiery sea, we held a gentler wind. Glowing with phosphorescence the waves came undulating through the night, to glitter briefly with the reflection of our green and scarlet lamps.

'Must be too far westward to see the Ushant light,' we surmised. Must I confess that we were uncertain which day it was, or how far our track had run?

What did it matter as long as we voyaged with the stars, watching them slowly swing through the night as they caught in our rigging for a while? Millions of light years distant they might be, suns in their own right, incandescent and fiercely burning – but for us their jewelled beauty held awe and mystery striving for utterance. Night and the sea were serene with beauty that was ageless long before land was born. That the heavens arched over men and cities as well as our yacht was beyond comprehension: there seemed only the ship, matrix of our world, sailing on and on, the night-darkened canvas curving in the breeze.

Dawn found seagulls flying near. The sea was different, paler. At length a patch of seaweed floated past, and then some off-shore rubbish. At mid-day a shadow brushed across the horizon, far to port. Speculatively we looked at each other.

'El Ombu,' I hazarded at last. 'The purple land. That's where the gods are steering us.'

We let the ship steer boldly on, convinced it was a thing of wonder to have crossed what seemed a great and empty ocean and found another land. Yet as the sea grew greener we forgot the lonely waters that had cradled us these many days. The ship, with the flood under her, entered a broad estuary. The waves ran small and brilliant, and a steady wind blew on her quarter. Soon the open sea was left behind, the shores came nearer, and the waves changed to bright ripples that presently became the calm surface of a great river. All that afternoon we sailed through a countryside of vineyards, following a buoyed fairway. Big ships steamed past. As the sun sank lower and threw a radiance over land and water, it invested everything with strange significance. At twilight, wharves and buildings began to grow on either bank. The lamps of a great city spangled the dusky sky. The water became black, shafted with arrows of light, and there were many moored steamships, their eyes glowing through the darkness. Beyond them the lights of a bridge spanned the waterway. Night arched black beneath the structure as though curtaining to-morrow. Quietly our ship drifted across the early ebb, nosing towards the silhouette of yachts clustered near a quay. The chain rumbled out, and the anchor splashed. Sails flaked down. We were at rest.

There the ketch lay all next day while we lowered the masts, for now we must proceed by engine under many a bridge and through countless locks. The noise of the city never stilled: voices in strange, excited tongue; clatter of cobbles; cracked bells clanging; roar of traffic in distant streets; tugs bellowing down the river. With dawn our engine began its muffled throb, and the ship glided under the bridge to make her escape.

Through a richly coloured countryside which could tell a thousand stories of ancient things we slowly moved along rivers and canals, lingering wherever fancy called. Poplars lined the waterway. There were broad vineyards, forests, peaceful fields and tumbling hills, browsing red-roofed farms, feudal castles brooding above deep gorges, and noble houses dreaming their ancient history amid the fields. There was quietness, dancing sunlight. Higher we rose with every lock, and each stretch of waterway revealed new enchantment. Birds sang from every glade; the world was verdant, newly born. Calm as the water sliding past our hull, the hours passed by and the weeks slowly mounted. But though we might stay moored a while, there was always the compulsion to journey on, for we were certain that beyond the horizon of to-morrow there was a harbour that promised fulfilment of our wildest dreams.

There came a tall aquaduct over which we sailed, and we stopped a day for supplies at a lost cathedral city. Then on and on, through a countryside growing more southern every hour. Towns with names like poetry called us to explore their mediaeval streets; tiny villages beckoned; tall trees gave slumbrous shelter from the mid-day sun; and everywhere a gay and voluble people revealed how lighthearted life can be. Even so, a day of sultry heat brought the strangeness of another city, and with it came uneasy recollection of crowded offices, hurry, frenzy, greed, disorder, and all the awful indignity of civilization from which we had escaped. Then once more the ship was drawing her slight wake across the surface of a new waterway.

Wine and song, laughter, quiet talk, high hope – oh! this was youth! And still the canal, with its avenue of trees, wound sleepily through a broad green plain across which drifted the sound of bells tolling the uncounted hours.

Suddenly the tall poplars and shading plane trees had gone. There were cypress instead. More hotly southern grew the land, and a range of blue mountains stalked the far sky. Next day brought a strange and thrilling citadel of shining towers and battlemented walls, set where mountain challenged mountain. In the magic of the moment we could touch the past – see troubadours, fair maidens, glint of armour, tossing plumes, and hear the rocks ring with martial feat and echo with a thousand sighs.

The ship sailed on. Inexorable her quest. Hotter climbed the sun. The land grew primitive, wild, unkempt – subordinate to the rugged grandeur of mountains walling us like barricades.

The last gorge, looming higher yet, became a tunnel, cavernous and long. The ship emerged to find six locks, all interjoined, and then a city hideous with factories and smoke. The tranquillity of weeks of inland voyaging fled. Was this reality? Did all dreams end in dust? Surely, only a little way ahead, was the rainbow's end: the lotus land we sought?

As though in answer, the mudflats ended in a blue lagoon tanged with the wild perfume of sea. Presently bridges opened to our passage, and there came a port where many great vessels crowded against walls each side of the waterfront. The harbour opened wider – and there, at last, we saw the sparkling Mediterranean and a cluster of little boats rigged with lateens, those romantic sails of the ancient world, the sails of Egypt and Greece, which came gliding towards us like a crowd of exotic butterflies.

'We must be nearly there,' we said as we stared almost in disbelief.

We moored to a jetty, close to the buildings of this harbour town. The heavy masts rose up again; shrouds were set taut; running rigging cleared; sails bent. Shipping her warps, we slipped across the moonlit haven and out to the silver waves. The shore lights dwarfed to glittering diamonds, and in an hour had vanished. Dawn brought a landless sea that gleamed like sapphire.

All day a warm breeze blew. The ship heeled steadily, thrusting at the little waves with happy purpose. Life was a song. The wind sang too, a softly urgent, thrilling song so steadfast that it kept the sails clouding white against the depth of sky. Throughout night the ship kept rhythm, steadily holding course. In the whispering silence under the moon, the soft song of wind and sea grew more mysterious. Night and my spirit grew one, and the moonlit sails arching high under the stars became the calm wings of our destiny.

But it was while I slept that the helmsman cried exultantly: 'Land-ho!,' and I found it was dawn, and that the loom of a distant mountain was lifting across the sea. Presently the rising sun revealed a coast of warm red cliffs and quiet coves and creeks, with golden beaches backed by pines, and inland lay a countryside of green and cultivated slopes with mountains far beyond. Every moment showed more clearly a little harbour, marked with a lighthouse at its mouth, and behind it rose a verdant hill.

Sheets were eased. Pierheads slid past. Within lay an anchorage lovelier than any we imagined. Its pool was mirror smooth. There were palm trees. Gaily painted fishing vessels lay sleeping on bright reflections. Soft coloured houses stood hushed beneath the morning sun. Though it was not yet six o'clock, men were already astir, working on their boats, and from the campanile above the roofs of mellow red, a bell was calling the faithful to prayer. Slowly we drifted through the crystal water towards a jetty at the eastern end. Wailing seagulls lifted on to wing.

Against the quay, an old black-hulled yacht lay moored. She hoisted a tattered British flag. Slowly her gaff mainsail rose, scarcely rippling in the gentle breeze. As we drew near, her white-bearded skipper called : 'You can have my berth.'

'We shall be staying many weeks.'

'I shall not return,' he replied. 'I seek a land called England where I long to lay by bones.'

'England?' we queried. 'Leave this idyllic place?'

He stared at us in silence, then unhitched his warps and hauled them from the quay. They splashed into the water. 'Listen!' he suddenly said. 'This is a harbour beyond the end of the world where life drifts by in a dream. If you would save your souls, flee from this place at once.'

Ah, but we were young! We stayed. Had we not found sunlight and freedom, and been taught the way of revelation? We watched him sail away and vanish in the morning.

Beneath the Cessna, the clouds had been steadily rising, hiding the mountains of the Auvergne. Then the white floor began to thin, and through rifts I could see a burned and arid land. A blue shadow far on the south-west horizon began to loom higher and became the eastern wall of the great Pyrénées. I realized we had drifted a little west, but this did not matter for it gave welcome opportunity of renewing acquaintance with the coastline of the Languedoc before searching for that harbour in Provence where youth had spent so memorable a summer.

In a long diffused line the cloud layer suddenly ended, just as the Met. man had said. Ahead, and on either side, spread the sunlit blue Mediterranean, dramatically contrasting with rain-swept England. I reset power, and on a long slant headed for the coastline. In fifteen minutes we were there – and horrified! Instead of the primitive, empty, enthralling shore, the French had built a seemingly never ending promenade of buildings like vast boxed honeycombs to house swarm upon swarm of holiday-makers. Only the distant rocky Catalan coast south of Perpignan retained its untouched natural charm. For the rest it was a shattering man-made creation, where mountains of soil have been moved and the vast new resort of Lecate-Barcarés created in all its urban horror. Even the volcanic Cap d'Agde had been refashioned and now sprawled with unvarying cubist boxes, and half way to Marseilles the Embouchure de l'Aude, and even the mountain area of Gruissan near Narbonne, were already suffering the ravishment of developers.

Houses, hotels, more houses, new roads – the wild sea beauty almost gone and only the inland areas, backed by their mountains, remained relatively unspoiled. Hardly recognizing Sète, I circled where we long ago emerged from our rural voyage through the canals and regained the salt surge of the seas. Turning the Cessna east, I headed high across the Rhône mouth to strike the land beyond Marseilles and find that long cherished, lovely little harbour of Cassis. But as with the rest, it had become a different coast, strung with unending villas and hotels crowding every available area all the way to Toulon. From three thousand feet I could not find our harbour. I dropped lower and returned towards Marseilles. True there were a multitude of indentations packed with boats among the procession of interlinked coastal villages – but which, oh which was Cassis? I gave it up, called Marignane Airport at Marseilles, took my place in the air queue, and came rumbling down to the stark main runway under blue skies of disillusion to join the heat and turmoil of the great city where we would dismiss all thought of visiting Cassis – for it is better to remember dreams.

13 Call the Tune

We had flown an ancient borrowed Auster to St. Merryn in Cornwall. Two days later it was imperative to fly Sam back to Dorset for a meeting at his Works, but on ringing up I found that Met. reported a south-west gale and ten-tenths low overcast. All the high ground of Bodmin Moor, Dartmoor and Exmoor was hidden by cloud, and I had no radio, so the direct course of an hour's flight was impossible. But I was well acquainted with the north coast of the West Country and thought that if I flew round it to Minehead I could make my way along the low-lying vale between the Brendon and Quantock Hills to Taunton, and thence through the flat Somerset countryside to Yeovil aerodrome.

We boarded the Auster, and two men held down her swaying wings while I ran the engine in the teeth of a gale that gusted up to 40 m.p.h. A wave of the hand, full throttle, and she was airborne in twenty yards rocking and lurching.

Sam wore a determined grin. 'You're going to get some

109

exercise,' he said, watching the jerky movements of control. Next moment we grazed the sullen ceiling of dark cloud at a mere four hundred feet. I would have landed back but for the risk of the machine blowing over. Instead, we headed for Padstow Bay, with ground a mere two hundred feet below us, skimmed the broad estuary of the River Camel, turned wide of craggy Pentire Point where white-capped seas surged in from afar to break in vertical cascades against its granite cliffs, and began to race on the the arms of the gale, downwind along the black and threatening northern shore. There were swift glimpses of little rock-bound fishing ports and coastal moorlands sloping steeply to the clouds which hemmed us over the edge of the sea. The ocean wind in full career tore the wave tops into sheets of flying spray. Enveloped in the din of the engine, we were interlopers in a scene of nature's desolation, and yet we had a sense of domination. We were held in suspense above time and emptiness, yet each of us was the centre of our private world around which all relationships and emotions revolved. As we surged along that shore, lifting and dropping, we were captive in a canvas-covered box, sustained in the turbulent air by insubstantial wings of wood and fabric tied to the fuselage by slender, straining metal struts. Each jolt seemed transmitted through my body – yet there was sense of full control both of the aeroplane and our destiny, despite the awe-inspiring impact of ocean vastness and solitude and the danger of that tumultuous sea.

Tintagel with its broken isthmus and remnants of a Norman castle swept under wing, and for a moment we saw the ravine-like shelter of Boscastle Harbour; then came the highest cliffs of all rising seven hundred and thirty feet into cloud, followed by an immense landslip and the long expanse of Widemouth Bay leading northward to Bude, the great cliffs of submarine larva having sunk to flat shore reefs, sands, and low cliffs before climbing again to form the tall stratified rock cliffs of North Devon – their tops, the barest way inland, still lost in cloud.

'Not too good, Sam;' I said.

As we neared Morwenstow our aeroplane was level with the cliff edge that rose darkly above the attacking waves like a stark black rampart. I edged a little further out to clear Damehole Point protruding beyond Hartland Quay. And there, a mile beyond it, was Hartland Point and its lighthouse, where the land turned an abrupt right angle to form the seaward arm of Barnstaple Bay. I banked the Auster round it, well out to sea, confident that soon there would be a lower shore and that the big airfield on the edge of the River Taw was within reach if the weather worsened.

'Sam,' I said, 'in the days of sail there was an oft quoted warning "From Harty Point to Lundy Light is sailors' grave by day and night". It's a kind of boundary line where the ocean waters of the Atlantic and the landborne waters of the Bristol Channel meet. Outward bound there is all the West before you, and homeward bound you know that you are almost there.'

At that moment there was a jolt far greater than any we had experienced. It felt as though the wings had fallen off. Without changing attitude, the aeroplane dropped vertically like a stone. Instinctively I opened the engine to full power and pulled the nose into climb – but to no avail. Instantly we were half-way below the cliffs. A great hand was forcing us flatly down. Coldly I realized we were going to hit the sea. There was no sense of fear. It was merely the unreal end. The water was a maelstrom of pyramidal waves where tide and wind fought each other, and the surface was flecked with lines of foam in every direction. Sam was holding on to his seat. The wheels seemed about to hit the water, though we were probably fifty feet high, when I suddenly realized we were not going to touch after all, and the machine was slowly, painfully, pulling upward. We sat there rigidly waiting. Once more the cliff top drew level.

'I've finished my prayers,' said Sam. 'I reckon we dropped all of four hundred feet.'

'Sorry, Sam.'

We had whistled along the cliffs so easily down-wind that I

hardly expected there would be such a tremendous overfall when the cliffs became a weir across that terrific wind. My old sailor grandfather used to tell me that many a ship got dismasted off Hartland Point. It must have been for the same reason that we dropped so viciously. They would be running before the gale like us, and suddenly the wind would take their sails aback as it cascaded over the edge of those cliffs in a great vertical eddy which reversed the wind direction as it struck the sea. There are records of a hundred ships going ashore around Hartland Point, and many another sank, as that old rhyme said, between there and Lundy, caught out by the reversing wind and heavy seas.

We flew on, each lost in thought. Soon it was obvious that the clouds were too low even to follow the railroad from Barnstaple to Exeter; nor after our experience at Hartland did I feel it safe to fly along the lee side of the long cross-wind line of cliffs between Ilfracombe and Minehead in order to reach that easier route to Yeovil. So we landed at Braunton. Sam phoned his office. 'No hurry,' he was told. 'The meeting has been postponed.'

The rest of the day we stayed at Barnstaple. While we idled away the afternoon I told Sam of the coincidence of how between the wars I found my sailor grandfather's first ship at Braunton Pill nearby. A quarter of a century earlier he would sometimes take me for a walk along the dusty road that led from his pungent, tarry smelling sail-making premises past several tall mills and warehouses at the edge of the river, whose brief quay and berths comprised the port of Truro. Beyond these buildings the unmade track wandered near the water's edge, and in half a mile came within sight of a great floating raft of oak logs, some acres in extent, 'pickling' as I was told. They gave momentary interest, for the lane proved a little tedious to a small boy, but presently we would arrive at fields spangled with buttercups and ox daisies marking a bend in the muddy shore, half way to Malpas. This was Sunny Corner, and here in 1871 the sixty-ton fore-and-aft schooner *Alpha* was built in the open, in the universal manner at that day. Charles Dyer was her master builder, and she was ordered by C. B. Kelway who ran her in the North Atlantic trade to America for fruit, and to Newfoundland to bring back salted cod for European markets. When a dozen years had passed, and the Portuguese with their larger Tagus schooners were undercutting rates, the *Alpha* was sold to my grandfather.

By repute she was described as 'a lovely ship', and fine lined for all her depth of hold. Between perpendiculars she measured seventy-two feet, and had a beautifully curving clipper stem with figure-head and carved trail-boards. With a beam of just over nineteen feet she was nicely stiff, and though her draught was eight and a half feet, she was able to sit upright when the tide drew out.

For a year my grandfather continued to operate her as a schooner, but altered her rig to a ketch for easier working. He then sold her to John Estick of Truro, who used her coastwise for three years before selling her back in 1888 to my grandfather and his friend Joseph Hunkin, whose son became the first Bishop of Truro. For nearly ten years she was used for coastal trading, and then was bought by those great Devonshire sailors, the Slade family of Appledore, as their second ship-owning venture. Two years later they began enlarging their fleet by purchasing *Alpha*'s sistership *Ulelia* which had succeeded her on the building stocks at Sunny Corner.

In his reminiscences *Out of Appledore*, W. J. Slade told how, as a lad, he watched a great match between his father's swift *Alpha* and the rival *Leader* racing in a good whole breeze neck and neck from Appledore to Avonmouth. Great was the excitement and argument among local skippers of the Bideford estuary as to which would win. Even the curate caught the fever as he watched the two big ketches cross the Bar together and presently disappear round Baggy Point. He eagerly rode to Ilfracombe, and sent a telegram saying that both ships were passing the harbour and *Alpha* had a short lead. They were keeping clear of the sudden squalls off the land which a southerly brings, but soon the wind hauled westerly, and steadily *Alpha* drew ahead, arriving and docking at Avonmouth well before *Leader*.

For the next fifteen years, as one of the Slades' fleet, *Alpha* sailed the West Country seas, sometimes as far as Ireland, but chiefly round and about the Bristol Channel, taking shingle to Avonmouth and loading lime or coal from Welsh ports. Many a time she was sailed ashore in one or other of the small sandy Cornish coves, and there unloaded before the tide made again. After fifteen years of successful operation by the Slades, *Alpha* was sold in 1912 to John Cox of Appledore.

Twenty years later I was exploring Braunton because of interest aroused by Henry Williamson's books depicting that area. Hidden behind the village street I discovered a straight, very narrow muddy gut from which the water had ebbed. At its head, just at the rear of the ancient houses, were two black-hulled wooden ketches. The first and biggest had only a mizen mast, and used the stump of the main as part of a derrick. The somewhat smaller vessel was a fully rigged ketch, in working order, though her sails were stowed away. Even in 1932 to see such a vessel was to step right back to the previous century. It added to the thrill to climb aboard and walk the decks of history. When I scrambled ashore, I saw that her stern bore the legend *Alpha*.

'And what happened?' asked Sam.

"By then she'd had sixty-two years constant service,' I said, 'but next year she sank in a storm in Bideford Bay.'

'Like us?' said Sam, and he grinned at me.

I nodded at told him of the later occasion when I visited Bideford with my young family. We had walked along the roadside quay looking at the moored vessels, and were immediately attracted by the rare sight of a gaff-rigged ketch of typical West Country fishing-boat design, indentical with those I had seen sailing from Cornish ports in the years of youth. We stood there admiring her trim condition, and found that she was named *The Puffin*.

'You come from Lundy?' I asked the skipper.

He told me that she was used for conveying stores to that island, and we began to talk about boats and the sea and the sailors of Appledore, Bideford, Barnstaple and Braunton. I asked him whether he had ever heard of *Alpha*.

'Knew her as a lad,' he said. 'I could take you to the exact place where she sank in Barnstaple Bay. You come along with me when I go to Lundy and I'll show you where.'

Next morning we made the voyage. She had a large diesel engine, and only used the sails to steady her or should the engine fail, though its steady *pant-a-pant* belied the risk as we nosed down the River Tor and through the buoyed channel, passed the shipyards and sleepy Appledore, threaded through The Neck between the low-tide stretch of sand on either side, and crossed Barnstaple Bar and out to sea.

Instead of taking a direct compass course a little north of west, the skipper headed more southerly towards the line of cliffs beyond Clovelly. A mile off shore from Gallantry Bower he slowed and circled.

'That's where she be,' he said, pointing down.

It was calm as a mill-pool, the sun flashing silver upon the blue. Beyond the water-glaze of sparkling stars was the long line of coast ridging the horizon from Clovelly to Hartland. Remembering the way the Auster had dropped like a stone and how Sam and I had only just escaped disaster, it seems probable that *Alpha*, old with her years, had gybed, taken aback by the reversed wind of the overfall from the land, and had strained her old timbers so much that she foundered.

Down the long passage of the years I seem to hear my grandfather explaining that all this stretch of sea was the grave of ships and men.

'Why?' I had asked.

'That terrible tide-race, gales, the fog and coastal indraught. One can't tell exactly why.'

But now I felt I could explain to him why *Alpha*, first of his small fleet, had encountered disaster twenty years after he had

gone, and that it was my world of wings, which had long
replaced his world of sails, that gave the clue.

14 Music of the Great Grey Geese

Several years had passed since I flew to the Somerset shores of the Severn, so on my next flight, instead of the usual encirclement of Dorset's broad imprint of crop-farming Celt and his close-knit communities, I headed north-west. The hot summer sun steamed moisture from the earth. A misty, dazzling whiteness obscured the horizon, and the faintly delineated hills and valleys and silhouettes of trees were lined with hazy blue which flattened them and eliminated the progressive change of tone by which one judges distance. Nothing was recognizable, but time gave a scale of measurement to the misty miles I travelled.

I flew isolated, remote, the world forgotten beneath the pearly sheen. Even the scarlet wings of *Tipsy* seemed dull and faded. I needed to put in time for my annual licence renewal, and this was an exercise in dead-reckoning with the distinctive sand-barred mouth of the Parrett as target. We proved to be a little off course: instead, there loomed from the mist a great concrete edifice, and after a startled moment I realized this must be the Atomic Power Station at Hinkley Point: a vast monolith to modern man where until recently only the whisper of tide and wailing gull was heard.

117

I used to know that place as a silted little fishing haven in the muddy shore. From there to Stert Point, five miles eastward, was lonely wasteland – reminiscent of East Anglian saltings, haunted by pied shelduck, twinkling oyster catchers, flights of curlew, scurrying sanderling, turnstone searching the seaweed, knots rippling across the sandbanks. From the air I have seen a skein of brent geese which settled in a curving pencil mark on the Severn, and on the war-time seclusion of the Pawlett Level on the opposite bank of the Parrett there were often huge groups of white-front and pink-footed geese.

To-day, as I circled that area, peering through the mist at the barely discernible fields, the mud and sand, with the satin brown sheen of the smooth ebbing Severn staining the misty curtain, I thought of those encounters. The first time I deliberately hunted geese from the air on this western side of England was when flying a Spitfire on war-time test.

Racing beneath an overcast of cloud I had seen wisps of rain brush melting warmth into the last pockets of snow that still patched the uplands of wild Exmoor. Above the bare, brown moorland no sun gleamed. There was only narrow airspace between ground and cloud in which to fly, but within four minutes the threatening slope of Dunkery Beacon had been vanquished, the primitive wilderness had gone, and Tor and Torridge glittered like a forked and silvered serpent's tongue beneath my rushing wing. The tide had ebbed. I scanned the ochre sands of estuary and bay, idly wondering if any geese were still on the mudflats, for usually they leave in earliest March – but it had been a bitter winter, and there was little sign of spring.

Down swept the fighter, down and down, with slipstream thundering louder. Controls grew heavy with the speed. No longer did the far cliffs of Cornwall stand dominant across the west, but dropped in company with the aeroplane, sinking behind the stark rock cliff of Hartland Point as though the seas had swallowed them. The wide estuary of Bideford Bay flung up at me, and as I flattened level at a hundred feet, the horizon closed in and became a rushing vista of sand-dunes and mudbanks ribboned with glittering water. Every secret of the tide was openly displayed: sea-wrack, foot-prints, tussocks of salt-grass, rippled sand, bright puddles, a dead gull with wings askew lying bedraggled below successive tide-line marks. Lapwings weaved twinkling into the sky, gulls and curlews clouded up on angled pinions; rooks and starlings rose beyond the saltings – but of geese there was not even a feather. So I pulled the machine up until it nearly touched the ceiling of unbroken cloud, and headed fast across the wide mud-stained waters of the Bristol Channel towards Wales.

On my left lay Lundy snarling in its tide-rip. Lonely guardian of the empty ocean, it swiftly slid by and left me flying with sense of disquieting solitude between shadowed steely water and endless grey of cloud, giving illusion of hovering stationary in an unreal vacuity of time. So I nosed the aeroplane towards the treacherous sea to gain a sense of speed. From the close contact of two hundred feet it still seemed a desolation of sullenly heaving water, the very abnegation of life. Yet in that instant, from nothingness, from the lonely emptiness, a gannet of startling whiteness materialized, flying with matter-of-fact confidence as it eyed the ugly swell. A moment later I realized that the monotone of distant sea had acquired a harder edge, and almost at once the far distance beneath the ceiling of cloud became low mountains, mantled with snow. Immediately the sea became impotent to threaten. With confidence regained the aeroplane raced like a roaring cyclone for the quiet estuary of Milford Haven. I banked round the great harbour, encompassing shores and fields and mudbanks with a glance. Nothing there: no geese at any rate, but many gulls and wildfowl. One swift turn, then round about and eastward until a few more minutes brought the saltings of two silted river mouths – first the Towy, then the Burry.

Jig-saw patterned with threading rivulets and twisting streams, these sequestered grassy mudflats could shelter thousands of pink-feet and white-fronted geese. But that day only gulls and hurrying mallard caught my eye. The geese must be far on their way to Spitzbergen, Russia, and the Arctic Circle. Dawning spring in Wales would no longer know the rush and whistle of their wings nor their loud and thrilling calls. Dispiritedly the reedy grasses of the saltings swayed in the sunless wind. The echoing din of my aeroplane emphasized the emptiness of sky and the barren air of those estuaries. Dwarfed and distant, the snow-clad heights brooded coldly.

With light pressure I lifted the fighter higher. Thirty seconds brought the soft vapour of unbroken cloud. Close under it we rushed north-east at breakneck speed, the coastline unwinding in ever diminishing perspective far up the Severn. Cliff and golden sand flung their miles away. Smoky haze of Cardiff docks and city momentarily filled the air and vanished. Where minutes earlier the Bristol Channel seemed unbounded, its opposite Somerset shore now indistinctly loomed, grew clearer, and begun to constrict the estuary into a tapering funnel from which the tide had ebbed except for a narrow channel twisting between banks of mud fifty times as wide. The empty river bed became an undulating desert of corrugated, muddy sand, mile upon empty mile. In five minutes we thundered so far up the river's course that the turbid water had dwarfed to a stream, twisting through the flat meadowlands of Gloucestershire.

Back we turned, following the opposite shore towards hidden Somerset. My sky vista showed that the Severn in ancient times trespassed far into the countryside. Only scantily was its former wide bed disguised by modern fields. Dominant among its hedged squares and rectangles was a long strip of saltings, set between two sea-walls, which riveted attention by its emptiness and size.

And then it happened! At the reverberating din of my aeroplane a compact company of geese two hundred strong lifted from the saltings and threw a half circle over the glistening mud of the tideway before landing four hundred yards away. There they stayed, almost camouflaged among the tussocks of wilted grass. I could imagine them standing alert, heads lifted, necks twitching uneasily in guarded expectation of winging escape into the unhampering air, for of all birds they are the most susceptible to alarm at passing aircraft. With other species familiarity breeds confidence that an aeroplane will do no harm. Rooks on the aerodrome rarely move for my taxi-ing as long as I keep fifty yards clear; surface-feeding wildfowl usually refuse to leave the water once my machine has put them to flight three or four times; diving duck rarely bother to swim a stroke, only submerging if the aeroplane skims within a few feet of their broad-billed heads. Geese, although so easily disturbed on land, once airborne seem to accept a circling aeroplane as another flying creature having equal right to the skies. They turn out of harm's way with so perfect an air of self-possession that one feels it would be an infringement of their code of manners and equity to make an aggressive move. So I did not stay near the birds on the Dumbles, but left them to their heritage of solitude.

Although I must have flown across those saltings many times before this occasion, only now did I perceive, as though with lightning revelation, its attraction to wildfowl. There was nothing fortuitous about their choice. This was no longer a drab and waterlogged field, so unimportant despite its size that it could be passed unseen in the vast perspective that is the concomitant of flight. I viewed it with the eye of an immigrant bird, discovering not only the rich prospect of food afforded, but the intrinsic aloofness from civilized fields, the promise of quietness emphasized by absence of roads and tracks, and the easy escape on a broad front to the impregnable sandbanks of the Severn. These were unmistakable physical characteristics. Yet there was more: a deeper insistence which gave to this lonely place a friendly air, and made it so palpably the desirable home of birds which had journeyed from still lonelier lands in the frozen silence of the Arctic waste.

Now that my winged encompassment of the Severn and its great estuary had proved that a few geese still remained in England, sudden conviction insisted others would be found not far away on an area over which I had flown scores of times yet never suspected the presence of such birds. But now I was certain, and headed the aeroplane towards it. The miles were a moment of time. The low estuary shore and fleeting fields for a few minutes were replaced by the city buildings of Bristol spreading into the distance, and then reverted to fields cupped by the shallow rise of hills. Below my left wing a low coastline of dull-hued rocky cliff lifted from a muddy sea. Under the shelter of a wooded hill, Weston-super-Mare slid past. Landward the dyked plain of Somerset unrolled. Seaward the water stretched far away towards the fading shadow of Wales. On my other side the Mendips lifted. Two swift minutes and I could see my objective. In the great curve of the Parrett's arm waited the broad meadows where I was certain the geese would be.

Down slanted the fighter, in ten seconds dropping fifteen hundred feet. Steeply banking, I followed the course of the river. Despite the aeroplane's speed, each little discolouration and hump of dull green grass gave an instant of intimate view, clear as though I walked there, but with a vista no hedge could obstruct. Even as I glanced towards the centre of the large treeless area a hundred pointed wings, and then another hundred and another, beat lightly onto the air. I stared incredulously. Yet it was true – the great grey geese were present in even greater numbers than I had foreseen!

Crouching in my harness straps under the centrifugal force that was pressing my body downward, I pulled the aeroplane into an even tighter turn. I was so conditioned to the engulfing roar of the engine that it seemed soundless, but the crashing echoes drove more birds and more into the air. Soon host after host of climbing wings filled the space within the orbit of my circle.

Skimming the hedges, and occasionally holding the aeroplane straight for a few seconds in order to fly under the geese, I slowly drove them higher. They were like giant snowflakes as I looked through the Perspex hood at the squadrons of birds thronging the sky above me. There would be a glimpse of white-marked face; a longer view of ivory rump and black-barred tail; here and there, to my surprise, a dark goose face which must have been an immature bird, for every pink-foot should long ago have gone. Up they went; great wings slashing at the air with perfect rhythm, mounting higher, filling the sky in every direction. Steadily the space between aeroplane and ground increased as I rose cautiously beneath the climbing birds. The extensive flat from which the geese had taken wing could now be seen as an isolated part of a broad plain which the river had severed with a two-mile loop almost to an island.

A hundred feet became five hundred and then a thousand. As the range of view increased, the great curve of river diminished to a small kink in a silver thread of stream. Soon it was dwarfed to insignificance by the broad waters of the Bristol Channel. Inland, the countryside lay inert and scarcely thawed, sombre from the ravages of snow and ice, spreading dull hues to far horizons domed with smoky overcast. Eyes ached from the speed and tightness of my circle. Against the grey cloud back-cloth, numerous great contingents of geese were separately silhouetted. Calmly unhurried, they swam the air with firm light strokes of powerful wings. Whether near in echelons and regimented ranks, or further away in smoky wisps and arrow heads, they filled a mile of sky, continually drifting and circling across my line of vision as they climbed.

A large group unexpectedly loomed beyond the upraised tip of my banking wing. In the brief moment before flashing past, I just had wit enough to roughly estimate the number, counting in tens. Their white face-marks and glowing beaks were startlingly clear as with one accord the marshalled force turned splendidly away. I gauged them more than a hundred strong. Scarcely had they gone than another group came near. Before they were lost I had counted each bird in a quarter length of their line, which similarly multiplied to a hundred. By matching the size of the other formations against those I had counted, it appeared that each comprised at least as many birds. Drawing a little further away, I scanned the impressive masses of flighting geese, counting the separate groups. Five, ten, I could see, and maybe several others, for they were dispersed at all points of the compass, and that meant more than a thousand geese had been flushed from the fields which on first inspection had seemed so empty. Presently they reached the lowest wisps of cloud and levelled off. Their inter-threading circles ceased as formation after formation settled into stride and turned tail on their winter haunts of the Severn shore, winging with calm purpose in a great combined force towards the call of Spring in those far lands that gave them birth.

I recounted to some ornithologists, who were familiar with the habits of wild geese, the story of my dramatic meeting. When I told them that I watched the ranked army flying into the grey distance until at last the geese wings became a smudge which vanished against the dark loom of the Quantock range, they seemed sceptical.

'But that must be south-west,' they said.

'Nearly south. . . . The birds flew east of the highest point on the hills. When I checked their course on the map it led as near as could be to the River Axe in Devon.'

They shook their heads, and emphasized that grey geese migrate northward when they leave their British wintering haunts.

'Are you sure they all do?' I asked, feeling a little non-plussed.

'Yes!' they said.

Though I found flocks of geese in Somerset and Gloucester on many a subsequent occasion it never again coincided with their departure from British shores, but I was interested to find Peter Scott recording in an early report of the Severn Wildfowl Trust, which now conserves the birds of the Dumbles for all time, that some of the geese he ringed there had been recovered at Kursk in Southern Russia. If those I set climbing high from their gathering point by the Parrett mouth had headed for the Axe and held course towards Cherbourg, they would intersect in mid-Channel the imaginary line of latitude on which Kursk lies 1,800 miles to the east. They could have curved onto that heading, and a week, with ample time for rest and feeding, would see them there.

As I flew through the mists of to-day I could visualize those birds again – the master flyers, the great ones whose powerful wings stroked the air with pliant touch and set it throbbing to wild music matching the clamour of their tongues: grey geese migrating in their hundred hundred, phalanx on phalanx! I felt at one with them, for did I not gaze at the face of the world in the same manner as the birds to discover the secrets of its estuaries and quiet fields? And I could do more. I could look far into the past and find the forefathers of these birds tracing identical tracks across land and sea. For countless years their flight along the whispering pathways of migration routes has been mystery, stirring mankind to wonder as they watch grey goose and crane, eagle and hawk, soar high over head, fulfilling the rhythm of life under compulsions beyond their comprehension. Given time and opportunity one might fly with the birds to their journey's end, so that at last the full and thrilling story of their secret air routes might be told with more accuracy than by 'ringing'. But what benefit would that be? Nothing measurable in terms of the profit-orientated economics which govern the world to-day – but it would be an enrichment of experience and the thrill of contact with the wild world of freedoms and constraints patterning the mystery of life and linking yesterday with to-day.

15 Wings Across Europe

The music died into silence: a crash of applause as the curtain
fell in rippling folds, then lifted to disclose the bowing singers;
fell and lifted and finally fell. Great chandeliers sparkled like
diamonds as light flooded the vast gilded Opera House, and in
a medley of chatter the matinée audience began to throng the
aisles. We hurried down the broad and splendid staircase
which kings and emperors and the glittering nobility of Europe
had trod, and so into the lamp-spangled evening air of Vienna;
we found the parked car, and headed past the baroque architecture of palaces and mansions, then through the shadowed
outskirts to the airport which was sheltering beneath a night of
quiet stars with a silvered moon lifting above the trees.

Flight plan to England was filed, and Customs cleared. We
walked across the floodlit tarmac to where Tommy's silver and
white Hawker Siddeley 125 Executive twin-jet was standing,
and stepped aboard.

'I'll get O.K. from the Tower and you take her off,' said my companion as we adjusted the head-sets and commenced the cockpit drill. It looked rather complicated to one who had been flying simple light aircraft in recent years, for the flight deck was that of an airliner based on electronic systems, with auto-pilot operation from take-off almost to touch-down. The selector push buttons were centrally at hand in front of the throttle console, above which were grouped engine instruments and warning lights. Within a few minutes the complexity of the control and instrument layout began to seem familiar. Our pressurized cabin was far ahead of the wings, the tips of which I could just see by craning my head, and the all-round view was good. Tommy operated the selectors on the roof panel and opened the H.P. cocks on the pedestal, and the jets immediately started their build-up, taking some thirty seconds to reach idling speed, transforming the aeroplane from an inanimate structure to the quick, tense pulse of life.

Tommy was calculating from a graph the take-off and climbing speeds at our all-up weight of twenty thousand pounds. 'O.K.,' he said, tucking the check list in its stowage among the charts, aircraft manual, and computing gadgets.

I released the brakes. Instant familiarization of the nose steering system was essential, for instead of being operated by the rudder-bar it was performed by a hand wheel on the left console, but easily manipulated if I rested my elbow on the arm-rest. I followed the perimeter lights, turned at the main junction, waited for Control permission, opened the throttles, and with the moon as company began to race down the broad runway which was edged each side like a city street with sunk gold lights tapering afar in perspective. They flashed past faster and faster as I waited for the critical safe speed, then, at a nod from Tommy, pulled on the control wheel – and the lights dropped away, the dark loom of the countryside spread wider and wider as we rose, sailing smoothly on the moon-filled night with its canopy of stars.

I turned on to the compass heading. Vienna, a few miles north, blazed with jewels amid the velvet darkness, and slid from sight, the music forgotten, the enchantments lost. Silence enfolded us, magnified by the light whisper of the turbines astern. Already the encompassment of isolation began to unbare new truths. I looked at Tommy – a transformed Tommy, a veil hiding his thoughts while he subconsciously stared into the night. And I realized that I too had changed. I was living behind a mask, waiting without urgency, at one with the night and stars, knowing that presently time would bring a calculated end.

Our course to Paris had been set westward between the jagged heights of the Austrian Alps on our left, and the lower, but older, time-eroded mountains of the Bohemian forest away to our right. A string of floodlit aerodromes at Linz, Munich, Stuttgart, and Strasbourg would mark our track to the borders of France. That was the kind of unworrying navigation I liked – leap-frogging across cloudless skies from city light to city light, with the loom of land easily recognized beneath the brightness of the moon: but Tommy preferred the scientific accuracy of radio and radar in finding his precise position in undiscriminating space, and secretly I was reassured by this sense of a chain of unseen people as watchdogs of our electronically guided progress. We climbed at two hundred and fifty knots, with power at ninety-five per cent, and were rising at three thousand feet a minute. At twenty thousand feet we levelled off in order to maintain better visual contact with the dramatic scenery, rather than climb a further ten thousand feet to operational ceiling. Height lock was engaged so that a level run would be made with no variation, and power was throttled below maximum continous setting to maintain three hundred knots. I took off my headphones, for we could relax while brief time carried our winged cocoon across the six hundred and fifty miles of this journey.

The moon had been lifted by our altitude high above the horizon; it dimmed the stars with a silvery sheen across the sky but made radiant the great loom of the Alps lifting diagonally ahead. I looked into the pool of shadowy darkness below our dimly violet-lit cabin and saw a few scattered pinpoints of light from little villages and isolated houses as though they were the earth's reflection of the stars above. In a quarter of an hour we were passing fast and high across the glow of light that must be Linz, and the Alps had become a ten thousand foot glittering, snow-capped, heavy mass, ridged and crumpled like a sequence of jagged icebergs rising halfway towards us. We could see hidden valleys, chasms, ravines, pinnacles and rocky knife-edged bastions; even the forests of the lower slopes were clearly visible – but the depths below the steeply sloping sides were shadowed with mystery. My mind might insist that this mountain was merely an upthrust outcrop of the world's basic structure, but instead I was overwhelmed by the sense of a huge recumbent mass of primeval rock crushing and subduing the land on which it rested. Great emptiness brooded everywhere. Vast, primitive power reached down from beyond the stars, bathing the scene with an indifference that was neither hostile nor friendly. But the majestic mountain still emphasized that man was nothing, whatever he might dream beneath the witchery of the moon and beckoning expectancy of stars. He was insignificant: less than the dust of million upon million years that had covered the world's primeval barren rocks and at long last made fertile the earth – that earth lost far below, drowned in the shadow of night.

Onward we swept, rushing through the moonlit sky, traversing five nautical miles every minute. Our identities had forsaken us. We were part of the dynamic impulse that tremored through the aeroplane. From time to time we stirred from this abstract experience to check the instruments, engine and fuel. Only the needle of the A.S.I. and the swirling hum of the invisible turbines emphasized that we were rushing through space. As we passed over Munich I stared across a little void of twenty miles at the ever increasing Alps and saw the lights of Innsbruck twinkling half way up the mountainside above a snow line topped by white peaks frozen into unutterable stillness. Moonlight, falling on this cataclysmic upheaval of the earth's foundation, transformed it to the landscape of an unfamiliar planet that we were cautiously exploring, awed by its might and splendour.

'Arise, contend thou before the mountains and let the hills hear thy voice. Hear the Lord's controversy. Oh ye mountains and ye enduring foundations of the earth,' I muttered.

I became aware that Tommy had turned to me. 'What did you say?' he asked.

'Sorry! A phrase from the Prophet Micah. Could he have imagined a vista like this?'

'Magnificent,' said Tommy, and we lapsed into silence as our wings rushed onward through the night, keeping formation with the moon, now huge and calm and high, irradiating the entire sky with a luminescent glow beyond our port bow. I stared through the velvet darkness at successive moonlit Alpine peaks. That huge range, for all its misleading youth amongst the mountains of the world, had stood there aloof, severe, implacable, brooding darkly through aeons of time while men had lived and died and been forgotten: kings, dictators, marching armies, the proud, the poor – they had been no more than moths fluttering their brief moment in the lamplight; yet man, that atom of impermanence, had the fortitude and courage to overcome the silent permanence of that great range and scale its heights – and we, flying with wing lights flashing, felt equally omnipotent though in no way brave.

Away to starboard there was a crown of light marking Stuttgart, with the beacon of its tall Tel-Tower a demure star. Ten minutes later came the glow of Strasbourg lights in the dark valley of the Rhine, and the Alps were receding southward in still greater heights but by paradox seeming to become smaller as they began to form the fortress wall that guarded Italy. Soon they were no more than memory as we sped across France.

Though the constellations hung across us in a triumphal dome dominated by the white moon, the depth of space and its sublimity had changed – for without the Alps as yardstick our height made the moonlit land even more remote, and the faint pinpoint lights of men on earth were now so few that they were almost indistinguishable. A repose, a quietness, overlay France drowned in the dusky, blue irradiated shadow of night. No longer were we omnipotent, but had become scaled down to two specks of life, unseen, unheard, disregarded, jouneying across ghostly moonlit wastes of an unseen world. Or were we? I saw Tommy was talking into his microphone. He nodded and took off the earphones.

'Just checking with Paris Air Control. Everything O.K. Might as well start the long descent,' he said.

So soon? We had only been flying an hour and a half – yet that small haze of light almost vertically below must be Nancy: there were a hundred miles to go. Tommy reduced power. 'Keep her at two forty knots,' he said. 'They'll hold us in twenty minutes at five thousand feet and then I'll take over.'

Pinpoint lights becoming more easily seen: the land transforming to a clearer silhouette; the moon sailing a little more abeam. I thought I saw the glitter of the Marne. Then more and more lights, and Paris, thirty miles distant, casting a halo of fluorescence across the horizon. Steadily height was lost. Tommy was talking into the microphone. Flaps and undercarriage were lowered, and speed was held at a hundred and forty-five knots under powered approach.

'On finals,' he said.

Paris spread wide: the mass of street lights made it suddenly real. Buildings became bold and brilliant as we slid overhead: there were hard shadows cast by the lamps across pavements and roads, windows glowing, lines of cars speeding down the boulevards – people. People walking along the pavements; real people, where minutes before the moonlit world had contained only us; here was the firm, unmistakable imprint of mankind whom we had almost forgotten existed – here in their thousands, their millions, they teemed the city like ants. There they were – believing that the lamplight of to-day was their eternal world in which they were entangled, hopelessly accepting, or filled with fear, anger, passion, or coldly plotting and calculating the gain; but for most, their days and nights were speeding past while their ingenuity was wasted by false premises. Why was it always a world of conflict, of battling ideologies that were a pseudonym for greed? And was there no more than a handful of men and women guided by a core of common sense, humanity and humour, who recognized the oneness of all the varied forms of living things? In the confusion there seems only our own inner light to guide us: the path is our own and alone.

My eyes were on the flashing airport beacon and the great vista of runway lights to which we had been guided as though it was our destiny and not the work of unseen men interpreting electronics. Our wings passed across the threshold of the airfield. The aeroplane's nose was true between the twin rows of lights. Tommy pulled back the throttles and the engines gave a whining diminuendo. The last move, after all, was mine. I eased back the control column as the runway spread wider and close, and the tyres gave a scream as they touched. The machine slowly settled onto the front wheel as speed dropped, and became a terrestrial vehicle which turned at the next intersection towards the line of immense hangars, brilliant with light that shone on rows of parked airliners. We cut the engines, and the noise of the airport crowded in.

16 Take Thrilling Wing

I stood high on a tall windy hill and drew a deep breath – not because of autumn's heady breeze nor the enchanting view of sunlit meadows spreading far into the distance below. It was just a matter of mental and physical tension and expectation before stepping smartly into the unknwon – and at seventy-one maybe I was somewhat old for such a caper; yet from boyhood I had dreamed of this, of opening my wings and leaping into the air to soar away like a bird!

An hour earlier I had been walking the downland ridge when I saw a young man and a girl on the lower slope assembling the duralumin tubes and gaily coloured sail-like covering of a dart-shaped Rogallo hang-glider. I gave a hand while mentally checking the strength of the thin rigging and somewhat questionable fittings – but as the weight of pilot and glider was less than 250 lbs., one cable alone could sustain more than twice that weight, so there was an ample safety factor on the assembly if everything was correctly secured. Nevertheless the wing triangle of thin gauge slender tubes, similar central keel and tubular cross-beam, seemed none too strong, and would certainly collapse if dented in a heavy landing or if the glider was blown over.

The caution of a pensioned test pilot was still predominant, for I remembered the days of long ago when my boyhood ambition was to fly and I made a crude wire-braced biplane of bamboo rods, tested the strength by supporting the wing-tips on trestles, lowered myself on to the lower centre-section – only to be precipitated to the ground as everything collapsed with a splintering crash!

'Doesn't seem very strong!' ironically commented my father.

Six years later, as engineering students gaining practical experience at one of the aircraft firms, a friend and I used some of our time to design a 'run-and-jump' biplane glider with a more knowledgeably and mathematically calculated strength of structure – although it was primitively controlled by swinging one's body in the manner the Lilienthal brothers invented in what then seemed the unimaginable dark ages of thirty-five years earlier.

The theory was simple. Terrestrial man, unstably balanced on two feet instinctively throws arms forward to break the shock of falling. So does a bird. The wings sweep forward and down, cushioned against the air to tilt the body up, and lo! the bird is flying. It has set the wings forward in relation to the centre of gravity and so obtains an upward levering effect; alternatively by moving the wings fractionally back there is a nose-down rotation and speed is increased. Slight differential movements forward or back of one wing or the other give asymmetric lift and so induce a turn or correct a lateral eddy. But Otto Lilienthal reversed the process using fixed wings, and by hanging on crutch-like supports under his arms swung his body forwards, backwards, or sideways to alter the centre of gravity in relation to the centre of lift. We proposed a slight improvement through taking our weight, once airborne, by standing on the landing skids. Perhaps it was lucky we were spared the moment of truth, for the little biplane was never completed, and the wings for many a year hung decoratively on the wall of my colleague's room.

The dart-shaped hang-glider that was intriguing me on the downland heights had a simple but brilliant solution that completely altered the problem of shifting one's weight in relation to the wings. This was to suspend the pilot low down in a parachute type safety-harness or seat which swung from the centre of gravity, and by pushing or pulling a fixed inverted structural triangle in front of him, to which the lift bracing wires were attached, he could change the tilt of the entire winged contraption in any direction relative to his body, for this intrinsically altered the centre of gravity relationship.

Francis Rogallo, a scientist of America's Nationl Aeronautics and Space Administration, initially devised the apparatus as a glider-parachute flexible-wing research vehicle to investigate the possibility of utilizing it for recovery of spacecraft and boosters. The essence was to use a stable triangular wing platform projected in outline from two intersecting horizontal cones or cylinders, thus forming an arched surface each side of the centre-line, the flexible trailing edge conforming freely to the air like a sail.

The prototype had a vertical duralumin structure carrying an undercarriage at its base and a pilot's seat with inverted control column, similar to an Autogiro's, with which he tilted the wing system laterally or fore and aft. Many successful flights were made, and as far back as 1962 the N.A.S.A. test pilot, Milton Thompson, made a glide from an aero-towed height of 6,000 feet, descending in 3 minutes 44 seconds. The public had been invited to watch the demonstration and thus prompted many enthusiasts to make simplified versions, resulting in founding the U.S.A. Hang-glider Association affiliated to the Soaring Society of America. Soon there were 8,000 members, and more recently hundred upon hundred have followed suit all over the world, including Britain – showing that the old spirit of daring and aspiration still dominates many modern youngsters, who, finding the cost of piloting aeroplanes pro- hibitive, have turned to this new sport in their determination to fly.

My two enthusiasts of to-day were novices – husband and wife, and on this hill it seemed inevitable that their names were Jack and Jill. She was apprehensive, for Jack had only made five or six runs with his Rogallo on level ground. This was to be his first essay from a slope, though the small plateau they chose was not very high, but if successful he proposed to try from the top.

'Have you ever flown?' asked Jill.

'A bit,' I said.

'Spitfires and things?'

I nodded.

'Then you could easily fly one of these?'

I explained that they were rather different, but that flying them must be quite easy because the technique was simple, and all one must be sure of was to keep the glider pointing straight ahead and gradually push away from the pylon bar when nearing the ground, otherwise it would be like stepping from a moving bus and the pilot would fall on touching down.

Jill looked impressed. 'As you know all about it, I wonder if you'd try the glider first because I'm frightened of my husband doing it?' she said.

I seemed to have walked into a trap, but then realized that subconsciously the moment the glider was rigged I had wanted to try it. A year or two earlier I had positioned myself one calm day under a Rogallo in order to gauge the difficulty of lifting and holding it in position and found that one quickly became used to the inertia effect of its 30 lbs. mass while supporting it with a firm grip on the control triangle.

Jack was eyeing me expectantly. 'Yes, have a go,' he said.

So this was it. Why not? At least I had flown conventional gliders. I had only to run with the Rogallo and it would lift.

'O.K.,' I said.

They tilted the glider from its nose-down position and lifted it, still keeping a negative angle in the light wind so that the Terylene wing was blown into inverted curves. I strapped myself into the harness and its narrow seat, took a firm grip of the triangular pylon and raised the glider, holding it at slight positive incidence so that the wind could assist. As I stood there, rooks and jackdaws came swooping down on planing wings from the hilltop sky behind me, curved over a newly ploughed field beyond the grassy foot and landed there with a hop and sudden braking of swept forward pinions and down-turned tail. That was the way to do it! A light last-minute drop!

I waited quietly a few more seconds until I felt the whole thing was under control. The downland slope flattend out no more than twenty feet below – and yet it felt an abyss. I remembered Kronfeld, the famous little pre-war Austrian sail-plane pilot, ready to be launched in his long-winged *Wien*, and then his guttural command to his crew: 'Rr-run. Rr-release!', and found myself taking four great strides forward, my weight lifting imperceptibly, and lo! I was off my feet and sailing forward and down. No sooner that than I was at the bottom and pushing forward on the pylon: the wings steepened their incidence and with a far slower vertical drop than a parachute my feet touched the ground and I was standing stationary. From behind me on the slope came a cheer.

So we got down to the serious business – first Jack with four or five tobogganing glides, then a tense Jill from still lower down but finally from the little plateau from which I had launched. I had another go, and in that few seconds of descent was able to try a lateral movement and recovery, but was level only just in time to land.

'Let's have a go from the top,' Jack said.

Presently, having recovered from the struggle of carrying the Rogallo up the acutely sloping hillside, I stood on the heights and took that deep breath of autumn fragrant breeze. Judging by the trajectory of a handful of dried grass thrown into the air, it was blowing at some 16 m.p.h. I held the wings floating

weightlessly above me at very small incidence, for if the angle
was too steep the wind would tumble the glider backwards, and
that would be a smash-up both for its structure and probably
for me.

'You ought to know better than to leap off this hill,' one part
of me insisted, while another was jubilantly urging: 'You've
done worse things than this. Go on – you always wanted to
do it!'

I took two steps, pushing the sailing wing forward – and at
once was airborne. I knew this hill of old from days when I tried
to sustain a throttled-back big biplane on the upward deflected
wind, and later soared those slopes with my own small sailplane. But now it felt quite different. Just like a bird, I had
leaned my wings against the breeze and leapt. Euripides,
Aristophanes, Tasso, Milton, the Psalmist and many another
poet had dreamed this ecstasy aright:

'Of silver wings he took a shining pair,
Fringed with gold, unwearied, nimble, swift;
With these he parts the winds, the clouds, the air,
And over seas and earth himself doth lift.'

Poised, pointing rigidly forward, I seemed at a tremendous
height. The wind was whistling past and the coned wings were
making a loud rattle from their flexible trailing edge. Then
suddenly I found that the slope was speeding past just below
my feet and realized that I was dropping steeply. In fact where
a conventional powered aeroplane may glide at an angle of 1 in
10, and a parachute falls vertically while drifting on the tide of
the wind, the Rogallo descended at 1 in 4 – and that requires a
very steep hill. But it was an exuberant drop until the ground
came up to meet me. Once again there was that instinctive push
forward to hold off, and the next moment my feet touched the
turf and we settled. I tilted the apex of the glider onto the grass
so that the wind held the sail-wing firmly down, then untangled
myself from the harness.

Three minutes later Jack and Jill breathlessly arrived. 'It
was beautiful – beautiful!' they shouted.

'It was,' I agreed, 'but I truly think it's too far down for you to try until you've gained more experience at lower heights. There seems a risk that in an increasing wind like this you would find it difficult to control directionally, for one of the dangers is that you could drift sideways on the wind and go headlong into the hillside. So I advise you to first become familiar with making turns to be sure of recovery in a gust.'

They looked both relieved and disappointed, but we carried the glider back to the nursery ledge, and there they each made another half-dozen jumps attempting slight changes of direction just as I had.

'I thing we had better call it a day before anything gets broken,' said Jill.

'Yes,' said Jack, 'but I feel pretty confident I could now make it from the top.'

'Wisdom dictates another day,' I said.

'Another day,' Jill echoed.

We de-rigged the glider and I continued my walk glad of this little adventure which threw new insight on all those nineteenth century pioneers and their emulators who turned their aspirations into science and braved with personal experiment the unknown skies to conquer space on fragile artificial wings.

17 Water Music on a Far Shore

From the cool shade of pines fringing mirror-smooth water that glittered under the summer sun of blue Canadian skies, I watched distant sails of a dinghy fleet drifting along the far shore of a lake so vast that it vanished over the horizon. I could feel no breath of wind, nothing stirred, yet in an hour those sails had passed from sight, and the lake lay undisturbed, ageless and still. All around its shores the firs were dominant, interspersed with silver birch. When I looked behind me at the russet aisles of tall straight trunks, among which the sunlight filtered through a shadowed canopy of branches, there was infinite silence, an ageless air of mystery as though time, as in every wild place, brooded deep secrets. I recollected forgotten boyhood imaginings of stealthy Indians moving like melting shadows along the forest track; of otters in the stream nearby, and beavers gnawing logs and branches to make their lodges; the howl of a wolf, and startled wild deer motionless and scarcely discernible among the dapple carpet of pine needles and grasses. Maybe it was really like that a long life's span ago; but when I flew next day above the lake I found that far around one end of its indented shores, hidden among the forest trees, were buildings – log cottages, painted clap-board houses and bungalows – a vacation township that attempted to recapture the wilderness as an escape from city life, and almost succeeded, with the aid of fridges, cookers, laid-on electricity and piped water. Yet the other end, forty miles on, was tenanted only by bird and beast and insect and an occasional leaping fish. It was as though I had discovered the outpost of a new country when I alighted there with a little two-seat amphibian Volmer flying-boat.

We had taken off from an airfield a hundred miles away. The Volmer was a strut-braced shoulder-wing monoplane devised for construction by amateur craftsmen. Its owner had spent three years building the strong plywood box-hull, welding up the conventional fabric-covered tail surfaces, fitting the ready-made thirty-six foot span wings from a standard Piper light aeroplane, and installing a stock 100 h.p. Continental aero engine mounted as a pusher on a steel trestle-strut mounting above the centre-section. Forward of the leading edge was a comfortable two-seat, side-by-side cabin with wide windscreen and hinged Perspex roof. Controls were conventional except for a long, spring-assisted hand lever between the seats with which to rotate a transverse cross-beam carrying external cantilever undercarriage legs, so that the wheels could be swung clear of the water. Stubby pontoons at each wing-tip stabilized the machine when afloat. Painted a yacht-like white, the trim *Water Sprite*, as it was named, was an elegantly attractive little flying-boat which gave immediate confidence because its design, though very old fashioned, was of long-proved acceptability.

In pre-war days I had flown a somewhat similarly arranged, but slightly larger British amphibian, the four-seat Saro *Cutty Sark*; but it had a splendid metal hull and tapered cantilever wing, and because it was designed to operate from the choppy waters of the Solent had remarkable seaworthiness. That was one of the things I hoped to discover with the Volmer, for I had long dreamed of the possibility of building one for use in the wide waters of Poole Harbour where I kept my small cruising sloop – but it could be remarkably rough there. It was particularly open to winds which soon stirred a sharp lop that might be difficult for a little flying-boat, causing it to cascade sheets of spray and buck and plunge uncomfortably or even bounce into the air prematurely. Flying-boats and seaplanes give particular

141

delight, but they need handling carefully. One of the fascinations is that the wind and run of sea and tide create such varying combinations that no two take-offs and landings are ever the same – nor, for that matter, is the approach of a yacht under sail to a mooring buoy.

Even getting a flying-boat into position for take-off has its complexities, for the wind may be ahead, astern, or abeam, and the tide flowing with the machine or against it or quartering. A small water rudder, which in the case of the Volmer acted also as a tail-skid, is provided for steering, but there are moments when it needs augmenting with the air rudder, and this can only be done with bursts of powered slipstream as it is otherwise ineffective at taxi-ing speeds. The complexities then increase, for this not only creates a torque reaction which puts a tip float into the water, but it can increase forward speed dangerously in a crowded waterway, particularly if manoeuvring has been half hearted and indecisive. It is much easier if there is an engine on each wing, for turns can then be initiated using one and checking with the other. In any case, down-wind turns in very strong winds can be risky, and often it is best to throttle back and let the wind drift the flying-boat backwards, or even sideways, to the required starting point in a manner know as 'sailing'.

Like all flying-boats, the Volmer's high engine mounting was essential to keep the propeller clear of cascading water, and it was particularly well placed in a central position so that the hull acted as a shield. However, so high a location produces a considerable couple between thrust-line and centre of drag, resulting in a nose-pitching tendency; though this can be partly compensated by the slipstream if the tailplane is set high on the fin, and partly by a somewhat aft C.G. – but if power is suddenly cut, the nose tends to rise, and this could be dangerous near the stall. So, with flying-boats, one pushes the control column forward before closing the throttle, and on opening up the engine the stick is eased back instead of conventionally raising the tail to flying position.

As I opened the throttle to taxi *Water Sprite* across the airfield into position for its landborne take-off, I thought I could just feel the nose-down effect of power, so on turning into wind I kept the elevator neutral as we gathered speed across the summer-burnt worn grass. She needed right rudder to hold her straight, but found her own longitudinal trim, and after a run of some two hundred yards, a slight tug on the controls sailed her into the air in an easily held shallow climb. The gently undulating, occasionally heavily fenced Canadian landscape was revealed sparse and bare, but limitless compared with little fields of England lined with trees and hedgerows.

I tried the controls. She flew much like the Piper which used the same wing, but the ailerons were surprisingly heavier, due, I imagined, to greater vertical inertia of engine and hull. Longitudinally she was nicely stable, and could be trimmed level with a mechanical tab setter. In fact she handled much like a car, and gave the same air of assurance: nor was the cabin unduly noisy compared with a conventional aeroplane having a nose engine.

Engrossed in *Water Sprite's* behaviour we sped the miles at two thousand feet above a countryside of homestead farms and rough scrubland pasture. Presently we reached the edge of a rugged, wide, forested land interspersed with primitive open areas revealing yellow-lichened, rounded rocks that were the residue of the last glacial age, millions of years ago. Here was the stark wilderness again – yet it was only an hour's easy flight from the nearest city. I thought of the contrast with England – that different quality England has from every other land: her gentleness despite industrial ravishment, and how her spell holds us all our lives – that spirit which has outlived all tyrannies and wars, and which will, I hope, outlive the greed and vulgarites of the present.

I looked down from our amphibian's ordered cabin at the New World wilderness below: the old, old New World. There it spread untamed, magnificent, attractive – and there, over the horizon behind us, was humanity struggling away from it, finding in crowded cities a refuge from solitude, intent on marching in step with others in the day to day struggle to exist, which has become an unending preoccupation with wordly success. Instead of harmony with nature, life has become a thing of concrete, plastics, and metal, and the long-proved creeds and loyalties of the past no longer guide increasingly restive masses of mankind, whose god is money. But we come with nothing, and with nothing we leave.

Sometimes there is a moment when the mind demands an evocation of the land without cities – the wilderness; and here it was below us, spread far and wide around our droning flying-boat. This was one of those occasions when one spiritually escapes from the mortality of life – one of the moments of grace. Yet down there, in that blue-green forest through which the wind was lightly playing, and among the scrub and rocks, by the course of the glittering rivers and waterfalls, everywhere was a prodigality of wild life, of beasts and insects and birds, of trees and plants, all counterbalanced, as for us, by the inimical forces of death in their competition for life.

Far ahead stretched a panorama of undulating continuous forest, the conifer tops spiky as a hedgehog's back. Here and there a lake glistened like a splash of quicksilver among the gently tumbling carpet of trees. Time sped by.

My companion was pointing: 'There is our lake,' he said.

I saw that it was huge, stretching far into the distance, set with islands like great ships floating on its surface, and its shores were indented into many bays and inlets. We flew high across the scattered houses, half hidden at its nearest edge, and began a long powered descent towards the invisible farthest end. The intrusion of man's domesticity was lost astern, and the wilderness of trees and water returned. Soon we were skimming at ten feet and found the water ruffled by the wind into sparkling little waves. On and on we flew, the trees high above us as we followed the western shore and saw the distant opposite side as a far blue line. After half an hour I discerned a wooden dock and a log cabin in a clearing by the lakeside.

'That's my fishing camp. Put her down right here,' my companion said, 'then we can run her on to the beach.'

I made a circuit, gauged the wind, lifted the undercarriage up with a smart heave on its big lever, and throttled back. Most conventional tractor aeroplanes when power is cut need the tailplane or elevator trimmer would back to relieve the stick load in holding the nose up; *Water Sprite* followed the characteristic of most flying-boats by lifting her nose instead, but was remarkable in raising it only sufficiently to settle into the correct angle of hands-free glide. That made her seem very simple to control, and the ruffled water surface made it easy to judge height – for with mist or glitter one has to guess, and this can end in disaster either through flying straight into the water or flattening out too high and dropping heavily.

'Just flare out a little, and put her on the water slightly tail down,' I was instructed. A moment later her keel rasped, and instantly it was as though she was jolting across a ploughed field – for the waves were the size of furrows, and the vee'd bottom had much less shock-absorbing quality than the *Cutty Sark* of old. Nevertheless the metal spray-shield strip on the hull chines prevented water obliterating the view.

She surged to a stop. 'Bit rough,' I said.

'Oh! She's O.K. on that,' said her owner. 'Try a take-off.'

Running attitude is critical with any flying boat, for the water-borne distance can be considerably worsened if the nose is held too high or low, or if too quick a haul-off is attempted. As power came full, I again felt the thrust push down the nose, so pulled back the stick to compensate – but she seemed to wallow, and the little waves hit her with hard thuds. One wing had dropped under propeller torque, and I was lifting it with an aileron and trying to hold her straight on rudder without inducing skid.

'O.K., O.K.!' muttered my companion. 'She'll be over the hump in a moment.'

Already we had run rough-shod almost as great a distance as this morning's take-off from the airfield. Slowly she accelerated into level attitude, and began her hydrodynamic lifting. A sheet of spray cascaded either side, and the wave tops impacted in a series of jolts, gradually softening. I could feel the wings taking the weight. The A.S.I. crept up: forty, fifty, sixty. The keel rasped more lightly. She was ready: poised: expectant. I pulled back on the control, and she lifted onto the breeze, sustained in a steady climb of seven hundred feet a minute at 78 m.p.h. as she passed the tall pine tops and headed towards the head of the lake a mile or so on. I brought her round in a wide curve, throttled, and gauged her glide for another touch-down by the wooden dock. The wind had raised no greater lop, but those twelve-inch waves seemed brutal treatment on her plywood bottom, though she gave no sign of bouncing. Her owner was quite unconcerned.

'Put the undercart down,' he said, as *Water Sprite* floated towards the shore. 'Then taxi right up the beach.'

The wheels locked down. I turned her hard aport, and she boated to the shore, felt the shingle under her tyres, and clambered, dripping, out of the water. In the lee of a spur of the woods I cut the motor, and the silence of whispering trees flooded in as we lifted the hood.

'Wasn't that a bit rough for her?' I asked, thinking of the bigger waves we commonly had in our own lake-like harbour.

'She takes it,' he said with confidence. 'Never let me down – though I keep that small speed-boat ready just in case there's engine trouble. Don't want to get stranded on these fishing expeditions.'

I sat by the water while he made a pot of coffee on the oil stove in his small but amply equipped log cottage. The hot sun beat down on the glittering lake. I was glad of the cooling breeze. Unlike yesterday at the other end of the lake, everything here was full of movement, and the forest seemed a happy shelter of sunlit avenues of rust-red pillars domed with a high canopy of swaying branches. Squirrels were chattering and leaping among the pine boughs. Somewhere in the bush the chickadees were conspiring 'don't give a damn – don't give a damn', and on the roof a whisky-jack mysteriously appeared like a small grey shadow mocking with a foolish little song. I listened to the lap of water, the rasping of lakeside reeds, the wind ruffling the tree tops as though there were waves breaking and retreating endlessly upon the shore. Here it was, the world as it used to be: simple, unspoiled, unblighted, sublime in the tranquillity of unnumbered years. Yet through the murmuring silence I heard in imagination the whisper of long gone seasons, the flow of sleepy streams, the rustle of prairie corn a thousand miles beyond the forest, ghostly footsteps and dissonant voices, the far away hum of engines, the throb of a city, the faint music of the universe. I saw the Volmer flying-boat waiting discarded – and realized that the long arm of technology reached even here.

18 Finale on a Lingering Note

The year had started badly. Rising wages in every direction
had deeply devalued the pension which had seemed so ade-
quate ten years earlier. Not only must I cut down on flying, but
the yacht must be sold and my lifetime of sailing end.

Over the beckoning horizon we had sailed time and time
again, the whispering wind curving her canvas taut as she
swayed across the waves, spray cascading from her fore-foot.
There was that first occasion with the sun sinking in quiet
splendour, gilding the western waters – and that last voyage
ending with a tow to reach our mooring in a calm: in between
were many others of sunlight and long uneventful days, but
sometimes of perilous landfall, swift currents, fog, and winds
that failed when they were needed or blew great gales instead of
the easy breeze for which we prayed.

In the long years since my first youthful sail in a black-hulled Cornish lugger I had had a good innings, of which the period between the wars was best of all, with creeks and anchorages quiet and unspoiled, and yachts relatively few even at the major centres. But now everywhere is overcrowded, the lonely places packed, chrome-glittering plastic hulls instead of wooden masterpieces, speeding motor-boats uncaring of the needs of vessels under sail, transistor radios blaring, noisy battery-charging engines, and night's stillness spoiled with halliards slatting on metal masts – yet out at sea, remote from it all, there is still the unfolding peace that purges thought into happy isolation from the cares of the world.

Certainly it seemed strange not to be fitting out the yacht when spring came – but there was compensation of time for other things, such as yesterday, when Tommy rang.

'Morning, Squire! We've got to sell the Executive Jet,' he said. 'Business badly hit by inflation. Can't afford convenience of private travel. Will have to use airliners. What about a last flight? I've got to nip over to Belfast and back. Take about an hour each way. I'm at your airstrip.'

'Coming right away,' I told him, for this was a chance of flying near the stratospheric ceiling of his aeroplane – and it was a perfect day. My last high flight had been in a Jumbo Jet airliner to Canada, when for an hour I sat in the Captain's cabin while the machine travelled its multi-computer-controlled and calculated impersonal course high across the restless blue Atlantic – a method very different from the hand-flown and radio-less navigation of war-time days when I flight-tested the earliest stratospheric pressure cabin fore-shadowing the airliners of to-day. Vivid in memory was the first occasion when from 50,000 feet I saw Cornwall projecting into the enormous void of the Atlantic like a granite wedge breaking the force of the seas before they reached the soft mainland of England. I could see the water's restless surge along those rock-bound shores, and imagination heard its thunder. Soon there was no more land. The seas stretched ahead illimitably in a world of water that possessed three-quarters of the globe and surpassed in depth the mightiest mountain. I stared down at the onward roll of what seemed a vast contrained force that was the very spirit of the waters and their solemn, awe-inspiring, endlessness. But when I looked upward into the still greater void of the dark stratosphere above my head, I saw that, after all, the immensity of oceans was finite and circumscribed – for here, all around me and beyond imagination's furthest reach, was the infinity of a cosmography from which even vaster powers poured down upon man's little realm of land and ocean and all that they contained.

'We'll be back by lunch-time,' came Tommy's voice obliterating the split seconds of those thoughts. I dashed to my car.

Within half an hour we were airborne, swiftly climbing to 35,000 feet. Visibility was enormous: the atmosphere crystal clear. I could see into unrecognizable distance a hundred more miles beyond the visible sweep of Devon, Glamorgan, Hereford, Gloucester and Wiltshire. A light canopy of haze hung in the windless sky above each hidden town and village far across the countryside – yet though those semi-transparent grey-blue smudges denoted millions of people, they were insignificant marks amid the widespread blue-green and brown of England's countryside that lay unseen beyond the great arterial highways packed with hurrying traffic. Those million fields we saw, netted with lines of hedges, interspersed with irregularly-shaped copses and broad areas of open upland, became the real character of England viewed from the great height at which we flew. Yet I knew all that land remained a battlefield; a fight for survival because there are too many people for the natural resources; a rocketing exploitation which within the foreseeable future will exhaust the fossil minerals and blight the land in false pursuit of ever increasing productivity, despite the counter-demand for living space. All the signs I had discerned on that far-away last flight with *Airymouse*, preluding my retirement, had proved prophetic. Towns and cities had become even more emphatic with great cubical buildings, pill-box towers, and acres of factories rising from an urban sprawl. Each year nearly five thousand miles of hedgerow have been removed and more than one hundred square miles of countryside annually swallowed by more and more houses, motorways, factories, great quarries, large reservoirs – all to meet the swelling demands of an ever increasing population.

Tommy's voice broke into my thoughts: 'What terrific visibility! Look! That's Ireland on the horizon beyond the port wing.' As we looked across the vista of England and Wales towards Ireland he reset air speed and turbine thrust to give the hundred miles flat downward slant that would carry us across the Irish Sea to Belfast.

Descent in more ways than one, I mused. Half the world undernourished and thousands more born every minute; spendthrift waste of resources for financial gain; the swiftly approaching end of petroleum; nuclear energy in the dual guises of saviour and destroyer; the cynical exploitation of science; the demoniac drive towards the abyss of unbalance; the greed, the apathy, the spiritual emptiness.

I gazed down at the ship-crowded channels of Belfast's dockland, and the wide waters of the Lough; recognized Stormont; was aware of a few prominent buildings; but the overwhelming characteristic was the sea of slated roofs in row upon row of ugly, grimy, terraced streets.

We landed at Aldergrove. As we taxied to our parking lot there was sudden activity. Police vans rushed to the far side. Sirens blew.

'Another bomb alert,' said Tommy laconically. 'It's just the way of the world. We might as well get used to it.'

But although the quality of human life is being more and more eroded as we become increasingly divorced from the natural environment, spring still came with soft spears of rain, the April sun warmly brilliant above the hillside larches opposite my cottage; daffodils in golden pools across the lawn;

blossom surging over the garden trees and hawthorn hedges; bird song everywhere. Age could not dull the beauty and enchantment. A pagan song still stirred my blood. Impossible to believe that ten years of retirement had already gone, nor did I feel one whit older. When I looked across the valley the sylvan scene appeared unchanged; the sky was radiant, and buzzards still soared wide-winged across the copse: but instead of the age-old rural silence there was now the day-long rumble of traffic from the once quiet highway a mile distant, and there came the sound of axe and saw among the trees.

One may sigh for the lovely places that have gone, the lost peace, vanished people, and watch dismayed the changing image of the countryside and encroachment of the towns – but throughout history nothing has remained the same. One must return to the factors of one's own life, weighing assets and defects with detachment, or it becomes valueless. For me there was still a world of beauty visible from the skies, for I had no need to fly near cities or industrial expansion; the heights revealed the same great perspectives of local countryside I had always known; and the age-long history of the land from the time of prehistoric man to modern days could still be read from endless signs left by his hand.

In quiet celebration of my next birthday I flew *Que Mas?*. Sunlit skies replaced the errant showers, and slow, great cumulus sailed in procession gently across the blue. I donned the fleece-lined leather jacket of war-time days, and instead of my usual deer-stalker hat used an ancient leather helmet, for despite the sun it was cold, and I had decided to climb the little biplane for an exploration of those clouds instead of my usual slow ambit at low altitude.

Creaking protestingly, the hangar door rolled open. Trim and taut, the pretty little white-winged biplane stood ready. So light she was that I had no difficulty in lifting her tail and pushing her out. I chocked the wheels, checked her over, primed the engine, looped the seat harness over the stick to hold up the elevators, set the throttle, switched on, and swung the propeller. She fired at once and settled into a steady rumble. I climbed into the tight cockpit and, when the engine was warm, opened gradually to full revs, tested the dual ignition, and throttled to slowest running. Stepping out, I removed the chocks, then buckled myself into the seat. We were ready! Her wings were eager as we taxied out in a swirl of slipstream.

The wind-sock hung limp upon its pole. I ruddered round to give the longest direction of take-off across the grass. With what seemed a roar of delight she rushed tail-high into the air, and I set her on a steady climb as we headed towards the Wiltshire Downs. Up and up, the propeller a blur, the wing truss of crossed streamlined wires boxing the view of sunlit fields and tree-lined hedgerows that were dropping further and further below and becoming dwarfed in the grandly enlarging vista of springtime countryside – and then suddenly I realized that everywhere was pock-marked with dead elms, their gaunt skeletons like bleak reminders of the pollution and exhaustion which is overtaking the world.

But the skies still beckoned imperiously, and the grandeur of the rolling Wessex scene was no less magnificent. Higher, higher we climbed – the engine singing a confident note, the very feel of the rushing air apparent in the firm sensitivity of the controls. Ah! But this was real flying! Like a boat under sail, we were at one with the elements, not cribbed in a cabin insulated with windows from the whistling wind. This had the same airy freedom as a bird – and I swept the little machine into a curve just to experience the pleasure as I set course for the nearest great cloud, its base some 6,000 feet above the ground. I had never climbed *Que Mas?* so high before.

Presently the tall, glowing, rounded mass of sculptured vapour, whose very whiteness seemed solidity, loomed close beyond the port wing-tip. Still we climbed. Ten minutes more and we surmounted the turreted, pinnacled, tumbling top, and found a fairyland of blue-shadowed dazzling white. From 500 feet above the cloud I pointed the aeroplane's nose steeply down, rushed at an arching cavern and swept through into the blue beyond; we curved grandly round, the sense of speed intensified by proximity to the white walls; lifted across hillocks of vapour; skimmed through a bronze-tinted chasm; trailed wheels through the undulating whiteness of the top while tenuous misted filaments puffed erratically between the wires; soared in a zoom that took me to the topmost turret – then climbed away until that mile-long cloud was but a petal resting with many others high above the dappled, sunny countryside.

I stared down at the springtime vista. The hills seemed eternal, the good earth rich as ever, despite the elms. Was the land really being eaten up in concrete at the speed the scientists said? Were people so recklessly increasing that all that huge open countryside was being overwhelmed? It seemed impossible. I looked again. Scattered widespread across the vale were innumerable farm homesteads, and every sheltered valley had its houses – far, far more than in those early days. And in the distance, where the silver brightness of the sea edged the long, clear-cut line of shore, the townships of Poole, Bournemouth, and Christchurch had coalesced, spread wider, and were reaching far inland. Yes! I knew the visual evidence – but in this sky-world of exuberant freedom I was sufficiently remote to forget that everywhere is drifting blindly to destruction.

By the turn of the century, only one generation ahead, the world reserves of copper, lead, and tin may be exhausted, and even those of iron ore could vanish in less than a hundred years. By that time all petroleum reserves would long be finished, though they could have lasted four hundred years had they been expended at no greater rate than what seemed the enormous demand of the war-time years. There is sombre warning from that celebrated group of scientists and economists known as the Club of Rome who predict: 'Barring radical re-ordering of priorities, the world will breed, consume, and foul itself back into the Dark Ages within one hundred years.'

Soon it may be only possible to wing the skies with sailplanes unless artificial petroleum and hydrogen fuel quickly prove practicable. While wings can still be mine I echo the name of this little aeroplane I fly: *Que Mas?* What more can I need than these occasional excursions into the dream world of flight and the afterglow of quiet contemplation as I gaze across the valley and see the buzzards soaring. *Que Mas?* What more?